Generation Grit

Ida Banek

PASSIONPRENEUR
P U B L I S H I N G

Publishing information
Publishing, design, and production facilitated by Passionpreneur Publishing, A division of Passionpreneur Organization Pty Ltd, ABN: 48640637529

www.PassionpreneurPublishing.com
Melbourne, VIC | Australia

To my parents. For all the trust, support, and unconditional love.

Table of Contents

Chapter One

Starting with Grit

If life were a fairy tale, I would probably be a storyteller. But it is not. Life is a journey, and that is why I love to call myself a traveler. I was born in a country that doesn't exist anymore, in the year when the world's population reached 4 billion people and Abba won the Eurovision Song Contest. My parents were no different than the parents of any of my friends: they were all modest, hard-working people who were trying to feed their families in a communist Yugoslavia. For all of them, life was not easy, but the quality of life was equal for everyone. Hence, people were blind-spotted to notice the size of their actual hardship.

I was a truly happy child. I loved to sing and dance, and I used my imagination to travel to some amazing places nobody else has ever visited. My dad was a surveyor; so, for his work he had to travel across the whole country, which probably helped to grow my obsession with travel from my early age. I still remember sitting in his car for hours on Friday evening once he would have arrived home after the week of travels and I would be sensing the landscapes he walked through. I would keep the steering wheel strong in my arms, passionately envisioning the places it could take me to.

As any other child, I was painfully curious. While my parents were working, my grandmother was taking care of me and patiently answering a million questions I could produce in an hour. She was not a well-educated woman; on the contrary, she was taken out of school at the age of 10 in order to help her parents with the household and the farm. But my granny was really smart. She loved people and she enjoyed talking to them, so she used every opportunity to learn from everyone. Sometimes even from me.

During summer periods, my granny had always been working in the field in order to grow some fresh vegetables and support in a small way the working members of my family. At the same time, she was my nanny, the best chef in my small world, a farmer, and a teacher who taught me how to read and write. She has never been formally employed, but she has had many roles and has worked harder than anyone else I've known. From the current perspective, I could say that she was a successful freelancer in the pre-gig-economy, and I was her most loyal customer for years.

In my preschool days, I enjoyed summer mornings the most. Then, my grandmother would regularly wake me up to join her on our agricultural adventure. I had a small seat at the back of her bicycle and a large bag of goodies to keep me occupied while she was working the soil. But children's books and dolls usually haven't kept my attention for too long. I was much more interested in real-life stories and new places my granny promised to take me to visit "one day." My imagination was endless, and my plans for the future were never small. Before my teenage years, I had "changed" many careers. I was a ballerina, a florist, a firefighter, and a journalist. One thing they all had in common was the short tenure of my interest for each of them.

I enjoyed dancing in my early childhood a lot and I can still remember the passion I used to put behind the preparation of my act to be delivered before my family every week. The time for the rehearsed performance was usually Saturday evenings, just ahead of the daily news program. My parents, brother, and grand-parents were all in front of the TV that had to be turned off so that I could demonstrate the dance prepared for them that week. I was hungry for the loud applauding at the end of the dance act, and I was convinced that I was born to be a ballerina. But, as you read on through the next few pages, you will see that my professional career took a different route. However, dancing has always had a special place for many years, I have been asking myself: "Was it maybe my true calling?"

So a few years ago, I asked my mom as to how come she was not more supportive with that passion of mine and hadn't enrolled me into any ballet class. And pragmatic, like my mom would always be, she provided me with her side of my dream with the following lines: "My dear. . . your happiness was always my priority in life. But you know, on those Saturday evenings, you were not dancing your heart out to be rewarded by the applause of your audience. You were dancing your heart out so you could collect money for the tickets at the end of the show!" And that line has hit me hard. I have forgotten indeed that at the age of 5, next to a small balle-rina in me, there was also a sizable entrepreneurial spirit that has steered my career choices until this very day.

Passion and Determination
My career as a ballerina hadn't lasted for long. I had put a lot of hours of practice in order for my show act to be of high quality and never escaped the hard work. But deep inside myself, even

at a very early age, I had known that the real passion was simply missing. I loved dancing, but not enough to keep me focused and engaged in hard practice for too long. So after a month or so, I decided to move on. It was a summer period, so it was easier to expand my business toward the outdoors space where I discovered my mom's garden to serve as the platform for my next venture. In a very short time, I decided to become the world's best-known florist, but as my mom was not interested in paying me for the decorations coming out from her own garden, the whole business model turned out to be just a day-long pop-up store.

Luckily, my grandfather retired that same summer, and in order to keep himself busy, he enrolled into a local group of volunteers trained to support professional firemen during the hot summer season. My grandfather was physically in very good shape, and he enjoyed that new occupation a lot. Often, after his trainings, he would be telling me stories about his experiences, and he would always close each of them with the message: "Never forget to help others in your life, regardless of what your job will be. People are all the same, and when times are hard, we need to think of others, as much as we do of ourselves."

I will never know if those words have framed me as a person or has that care for others always been part of my DNA. But I know for sure, it was the summer that marked my childhood and bonded my heart and mind in such an unusual way. By now, you probably know that I was a child with very strong determination. When there was an idea in my mind, I found the way to direct my activities and then realize it. And as my grandfather's stories were too good to be true, I couldn't just sit at home—I had to join him in those trainings and directly observe as to how to be prepared for the fire to come. I was disturbing a poor old man so much that one day he took me with him under the condition that I sit at a distance during his practice under the strong supervision of my older brother. I behaved well and enjoyed the experience a lot; but already for the next day, I had a plan.

In the street where my grandparents lived, there were at least 10 other kids who were maybe a few years older than me. They didn't know much about the role firemen had in our lives, but I was ready to tell them that story passionately. So, I formed a group of those eager to be trained and prepared for the potential fire, which may harm people's lives. And I appointed my grandfather as our coach. I am sure he was not crazy about that plan of mine, but he was smart enough to realize that saying a no to my newly developed idea—would be much more painful than actually accepting the challenge.

The next couple of weeks turned out to be the most memorable part of my childhood. My grandfather had developed the training ground in our backyard where my mom's gardening equipment had turned into valuable assets for our fire-fighting efforts. We were all having fun, learning a lot, and becoming ready to help at times of need. And one day, the need arrived. I was playing in the garden on my own when in the late afternoon of a hot summer day, the sharp sound of an emergency alarm calling for action started. My grandfather was not at home at that time, but I stayed focused on finding my bike to step into action as I was ready to deliver the support other people needed. However, my mom had different needs from me that day and stopped my adventure with the goal to enroll me into the primary school.

Effort and Talent

My parents have not attended any college, but they were very dedicated in their mission to provide my brother and me with the best possible education they could afford. I always respected how much my mother valued learning (even at times when I felt harassed with her lectures on the importance of studying), because having a university degree was a dream she was never able to realize. For me, on the contrary, the sound of school and formal education was simply boring. In my simple mind, it meant that I would need to move away from my grandparents, leave all our adventures behind, and replace them with a strict classroom regime I was not ready to try.

Yet, the time arrived, and my mom took me to a psychologist as part of the regular enrolment process. My whole family was extremely excited about that day. I was a smart kid who knew how to read, write, and compute; but I've felt that since I knew all of that anyway, it would be a waste of time to sit in the classroom and wait for others to learn the lessons I had mastered already. So, when my mom left me with the lady called a psychologist, I took my chance to fix the thing. At first, I was polite and answered all her questions. I was drawing and writing everything she asked me to, but the moment she asked me how I feel about going to school—I gave her a bit of a lecture. I listed out all my reasons and clear facts as to why this whole school plan was not a good option for me, and I proudly concluded my elaboration with a sentence: "You know, I think I am psychologically not ready to take on that responsibility."

Then, my mom was asked to join us, and I don't remember well what the feedback she got from the psychologist actually was.

But I do remember her long, silent face on our way back home. She was convinced that I was a fast learner who always manages to find an easy way out in every situation, but in her opinion— school was something not to play around with. Formal schooling process was there to finally teach me a lesson about how hard work and discipline transform people into strong achievers. With all the potential she had seen in me, my mom was on a mission to secure that I become the strong achiever!

Honestly, I did not understand my mom much at that age, but now I am grateful that she installed that vision of "the power of effort" so strongly in me. What is talent alone, without sufficient effort that builds and transforms it into a skill? Some may call it unrealized potential, others say it's a missed opportunity; yet, I like to see it as a chance. And to take that chance forward is never too late.

But let's come back for a second to my school story and the fact I finally did not hate it that much. Over time, I discovered my passion for natural science, history, and geography. My natural curiosity was fed by amazing information about the diverse world around me, and my desire to discover it became a dream. I have been dreaming with my eyes wide open. I have never missed a single opportunity to regularly share that dream with my caring parents, but despite their hard work in multiple jobs they've held in parallel, they were never in a position to afford sending me on any trips. So, I had no other choice but to look for alternative solutions on my own.

One day at the school, I heard the story about a group of young people in my city who had traveled the world as a dancing troupe. I spotted my chance immediately. I always liked music and dancing. I was not talented enough to become a ballerina, but I was a determined, hard working kid who could put hours of practice in order to achieve her bigger, longer-term goal. So, I applied for the dancing training and then spent 4 hours of daily practice to be selected into the "A-league" of dancers, who were sent on world tours and who were competing in festivals around the globe. And I finally did it.

Just ahead of my 18th birthday, I held my first boarding pass for the flight to London, followed by a trip to New Zealand and Australia on a 6-week-long tour. I had never been in a plane before that, and I had not seen much of the world before that either. But the gritty soul in me had steered my efforts using just my average dancing talent to the point of changing my life for good. The rest is history. I returned from that tour as a different person with a clear vision for my future. I discovered my passion for the new, the unexpected, and the undiscovered, and I have never allowed myself to look back.

So, in my story, having some basic talent for dancing helped me a lot. But in my dancing group, there were girls with 10 times more talent than me who were never selected into the final team. My passion for travel had fueled my perseverance in the effort to keep training hard, which helped me to reach my goal. The size of my grit had beaten some incredible talent not eager to train. The grit in me was the reason I stepped into that plane almost 30 years ago and is the reason I can keep my flights at a high altitude for every aspiration I decide to pursue.

Yet, when it comes to the role of grit in our personal and professional lives, Angela Duckworth is definitely the person on a mission to help us realize its full potential. Angela Duckworth is a professor of psychology at the University of Pennsylvania and the author of the book *Grit: The Power of Passion and Perseverance.* Her diligent studies of grit and other areas that predict success in life have inspired my work with students over the past years too. I have found a lot of personal examples in Duckworth's theory as to how we get from talent to achievement. Talent, defined as the speed with which can improve a certain skill, is important—and there is no doubt about it. Yet the effort that we put behind building that skill actually counts twice in the whole algorithm.

Pathway to Grit
In this book, I will be talking about grit a lot. Not about its definition that scientists keep arguing about, but the meaning I found for grit in my own life. I have exhibited the passion and perseverance for my long-term goals in many different stages of my journey, and dancing in order to travel was one of its simple forms. But next to the passion, perseverance, and clear goals for the long run, I always had a strong self-awareness too. I knew what my strengths were and how much effort I had to put behind them in order to succeed.

During my education, I was always an excellent student. I was a bit competitive, so not being the best in the class was never an option for me. But more than anything, I was sincerely curious and eager to research and learn from others, so I dare to say that basics for good journalism were routed in me. Being a teenage girl, I was probably not self-aware; however, I became very passionate about the idea of journalism during my high school. I liked to research a lot, and I could have spent days in finding facts and reasons behind unexpected developments around me. Besides that, I knew that a professional career in journalism would have the potential to bring me some travel opportunities while in the career. I could picture myself in situations where I would travel around the world in order to find successful people who have achieved great things in life. Then, I would frame those insights into stories that others can learn from and thrive. The idea was larger than life, and I was dedicated to become a medium that inspires others to grow. But life has its twists for everyone, and it happened to me as well.

At the beginning of the 1990s, the civil war started across the Balkan countries, and it brought a different image of journalism to my attention. I grew scared of what good reporting stands for, and I didn't see all the needed elements in me for pursuing the career at all. I began doubting what I wanted to do, and I was reminded by my parents regularly as to why it was better to reconsider my decision about the choice of academic studies. It was wise at that time to explore alternative paths forward, and I started to question myself what is actually my calling in life.

When one is 18 years old, the question on one's life calling may be a bit blurry even for the brightest young person. So, I was struggling a bit, but then I noticed that my greatest reward was coming from situations that required solutions and from simple ways of dealing with complex issues. Researching and discovering were in my blood. Despite my focus on journalism for some years, I realized that I needed to find alternative ways to connect inspiration and growth for success. Instead of becoming a storyteller and a mediator in this world, I chose to actively support people in their efforts to reach their goals. The safest way for me to realize that aspiration in the country hit by war and uncertainty was the choice to study psychology.

I sincerely enjoyed my studies. Despite all the safety threats that were impacting normal students' lives, I was pleased with personal development, and I was still able to "dance my way" around the world. Over the 4-year period, I was exposed to various specializations in the field of psychology and was selecting areas of my strongest interest. Human behavior driven by our personality traits and deep internal drivers became intriguing to me and have steered my life ever since. At the time of my graduation, I knew how to discover individual strengths. I was trained on how to measure them, and I was eager to help people amplify them in order to realize their full potential. In all honesty, 25 years ago, nobody was talking about grit, but if I would have just begun my career today, I would proudly label myself as a "grit developer."

Unfortunately, we can't travel back in time. But what we can do is try to find paths that impact our future. When I think of years ahead of us, I always see the incredible role that insights into human behavior can play in helping us all to become better entrepreneurs, partners, team members, and leaders. I believe that greater longevity and ongoing technological advancements will build the world where lives are governed by algorithms and where professional careers will look like marathons. In order to be successful in that world, we will need to grow our grit as much as our capabilities to collaborate with human and artificial workforce. And my goal with this book is to provoke your thoughts about the future and invite you to help me promote the power of grit in the years to come.

Chapter 2

The War for Talent Is Finally Over

It was the spring of 1998, and I was in my first corporate job. Curious about the world and my future place in it, I was learning fast and working hard. I used to stay long hours in my office with great enthusiasm to tap into any kind of a given task that provided me with the opportunity to learn. One day, I learned from my superior that he had nominated me into the group of "emerging talents" to be developed into managers over the next couple of years. But to his surprise, I was not excited about that nomination and the program at all. I was actually full of questions about what emerging talent actually means and how shall we recognize people for that category in the future. Little did I know at that time that my simple question was actually larger than life and that we will collectively spend decades in the search for answers to simple questions linked to complex talent challenges.

I had a really great boss who wanted me to grow and develop. So in order to feed my curiosity, he decided to send me to a large HR conference in Italy that was called: "The War for Talent." I was only 24 years old, and I had no idea what that war was about, but I was really eager to discover all about it and then report back to my team on how to get ready for the upcoming battles. By the end of the week in lovely Florence, I was well informed about the new concept designed by McKinsey just a year before. And I was really excited to go back home with a strong feeling that this war for talent is actually not bad at all. Being green behind the ears, self-centered, and with zero business savviness, I was actually excited to see that in the future people will be stimulated to change their jobs regularly. It looked great to me and I couldn't wait for that new future to arrive.

Born in the early 1940s, my parents were baby boomers in theory. In practice, they were more than that. In their mind, there was no other way to adulthood and independence besides getting a good and safe job one can retire from. In my mind, that was scary. Only after a year in my first role post graduation, I knew that the bank that employed me as a management trainee will not be the one to throw a retirement party for me. The team I worked with was amazing. I liked HR a lot, and I was very good at recruitment. But the whole corporate setup, with slow processes and change-reluctant culture, was not my cup of tea. My parents were convinced that something was wrong with my brain. They started evaluating what they did wrong with my upbringing, especially as my older brother's career attitudes were polar opposite of mine. My dear parents tried their best; they were reminding me weekly that I need to slow down, stop dreaming, and wait a bit for that tea of mine to cool down a bit before I rush into the next tea party. But honestly, patience was never my strength.

The booming economy at the end of 1990s was generating a demand for highly skilled employees that was far beyond the actual supply. Just like me, many employees were seduced by opportunities to join other companies in order to accelerate their career progression, improve their compensation opportunities, or simply just try different things. Needless to say, that demand for good head-hunting services and for the science of personality was exploding. Being a psychologist, trained to design and apply various personality and ability assessments, I was in heaven!

Nurturing Talent
Talent became a really sexy word, and we all wanted to have talent, display it successfully, and finally monetize it. The issue was that for a very long time, psychologists were convinced how success in any kind of field or career depends primarily on the talent we have inherited and secondarily on the motivation we have to grow it further. So, in my personal case, I was aware that my dancing talent had its limitations as I was not "born" to become a professional dancer. So, my motivation behind the goal to finally travel and see the world was driving a great deal of my efforts at practicing, but I would have never thought of turning my dancing into a career.

However, through the 1980s, some large and very serious studies started to change our views on talent, its evolution, and opportunities for development. One of those landmark studies was led by an American educational psychologist, Benjamin Bloom, who studied 3 groups pursuing different occupations: professional athletes, musicians, and scientists. When Bloom's team started to interview 21 eminent pianists (who were all finalists of major international competitions), some intriguing findings started to line up. One of the major findings was the surprising fact that, in their early childhood, none of the famous piano players was standing out at the local, regional, or national levels. None of them had piano teachers with strong expertise or a track record of high teaching success; rather it was someone who was simply living in the neighborhood. But what all of them had in common was the number of hours placed into practice that was far beyond the average of other children at the same age.

The Swedish psychologist, Anders Ericsson, who is internationally recognized for his work in the psychological nature of expertise and human performance, has found in his research that in order to generate expertise in a certain field, we need to invest 10,000 hours of deliberate practice. It basically means that a child who practices to play piano 4 hours a day, 5 days a week for 10 years will reach the level of expertise to finally stand out and achieve some extraordinary results. But, who on earth would be willing to put this much practice into anything?

I can tell you that despite my desire to discover the world, I would have never signed up to place this amount of effort behind my dancing. And I hate to admit that I believe our individual grit may not be sufficient to turn us into stars. What can help us though to sustain our strong efforts (that will pay-out only in the long run) could be the external support provided by coaches, mentors, bosses, or role models who are keen to listen. So when we go back to our piano players from Bloom's study, we notice an extremely important finding that tells how firstly teachers of all the pianists were kind, caring, and very patient people. They were the reasons that in early childhood those musicians found piano lessons fun, exciting, and highly enjoyable. And they were the reasons why hours spent in practice did not seem to be an effort, but a joy.

We will all agree that talent matters and is important in anything we do. But gritty people with medium level of potential will be able to successfully blend their interests, goals, focus, and drive in order to achieve high performance. And when we add great leadership on top of that grittiness—the outcome can be short of impressive. As parents, teachers, coaches, managers, mentors, or simply leaders of various kinds, we all play a role in talent amplification. When we resist looking for talent first, and instead we invest time to motivate gritty people to work hard beyond their belief of what's possible—then the concept of talent shortage will simply become obsolete.

Talent War or a Myth?
While I am writing this chapter, the summer of 2019 is fading out. Swiss mornings are getting colder, and sunlight is becoming shorter every day. Twenty years after the war for talent has started, businesses around the world feel enormous pressure to supply the right quality of talent for their existing and future business needs. Low unemployment rates due to the economic growth over the past decade are shaking the recruitment industry, and when I speak to hiring managers around the world, 8 out of 10 usually tell me that talent shortage is their biggest business challenge.

But then again, I work with students all the time. And stories I hear from talented, young people eager to move into the workforce are not aligned with those expressed by hiring managers. They tell me about their frustrations caused by the lack of communication along the recruitment process, they complain about various negative experiences generated along the way, and they are frustrated with the length of time needed for the process to be finalized.

In 1997, when I started to look for my first job, Google didn't exist. Instead, every Saturday morning, my mom would serve me a jar of coffee and the most popular local newspapers to kick off my job search. The number of open entry-level positions was usually tiny, so my search activity was done while the coffee in my cup was still hot. Then, I would simply pack my short CV into an envelope to be sent out the same day. It usually took about 3–4 weeks before someone would call my landline number to invite me for an interview or about 6–8 weeks before a short, but professional rejection letter would land in my mailbox. I know that this may sound like a flashback into the 16th century, but that was the way to find a job a bit more than 20 years ago.

What makes me really sad is to see that recruitment timelines have not changed much until today. Despite the fact we have advanced search engines, e-mails, 5G networks, and various artificial intelligence (AI) assistants, our approach to hiring is often outdated and, in general, takes too long. On a daily basis, I hear stories from passionate, bright people on how they have applied for a role they believed to fit well in, and 5 weeks later, they still haven't heard a word back. How can that even be possible?

So, being in a position to hear both sides of the same story, I believe that the war for talent is over. Talent has simply moved on, and hiring managers get stuck with broken (or rotten) supply chains. In my opinion, we need to step away from recruitment as a single source of talent management frustration, and instead focus on 2 areas that have to be solved in order to create a future where talent can thrive and wars can be over. One is called *disengagement* at work and the other is known as *gig-economy*.

Disengagement at work became a pandemic that has to be put under control. Gallup's recent study has shown that only 33 percent of the working population is engaged in their work, which annually drives between USD450 billion and USD550 billion of losses in productivity within the United States alone. I mean, what kind of a result can we produce with only 33 percent of resources working in anything we do? Just imagine for a second, the guitar that has only 2 strings instead of 6 and ask yourself what kind of music the best guitarist would be able to produce.

But, we don't do much about this disease at all. For years now, we have known that we have an issue, we measure engagement year-on-year, and we continuously miss out on opportunities to install some significant change. One of the main reasons why most engagement efforts fail is the fact we don't put a detailed strategy in place on how to cultivate employees' commitment. Believe it or not, less than 30 percent of companies (be it large or small) seriously plan how to solve this issue. And where there is no plan, there is no gain.

It is high time to open a dialogue over this subject—because lack of regular, clear, and timely communication is causing the problem in the first place. And then, once strong communication channels are in place, there is no space to hide. It takes 2 people to dance and it takes at least 2 people to have a conversation. Both managers and employees share the responsibility in that process and are in charge of co-creating the future based on a strong culture of feedback. In my work with students and young people in their first jobs, it is clear that they are hungry for regular feedback and constructive communication. For all of us in management roles, this aspiration is not always easy to reach. Why that's the case and how to solve it will be elaborated in **chapter 3.**

Next to the improvements in communication, we can also do a lot to improve developmental opportunities people have in today's world. Career growth and development are significant to the incoming workforce and will only grow in importance. But somehow, almost 70 percent of employees believe that the opportunity for career advancement is so low that it's better to seek for a promotion somewhere else. And instead of providing those employees with tools to proactively drive their careers forward within their current organizations, we have allowed them to turn into "passive job seekers" whose careers are actively managed by LinkedIn and head-hunters alike.

The current situation is bad not only from the engagement perspective, but it consequently develops the culture of passive-aggressive behavior, which, in my opinion, is a fast line to destroyed accountability at the individual and organizational levels alike. Passive-aggressive behavior is often hard to pin down, but the most common signs that it's time for intervention are employees' resistance to openly discuss concerns, general avoidance of responsibility, and deliberate inefficiency in their work. And to be clear here, when I talk about employees, I talk about everyone. Managers, executives, and individual contributors are all employees in some form and are all in the mix of passive (and active) job seekers.

When I close my eyes and start dreaming about the future of work, I can see the world career management is not a process. It is not a single meeting within a year that is closed without actionable outcomes and it is definitely not led by managers. It is a rounded experience that employees drive on their own, and it passionately connects various stakeholders in constructive interactions every single day. That is the future I want to be part of, and that is why I will describe it in detail in chapter 6 of this book.

Time to Futurize Ourselves

In the future of work that I dream about, employees are engaged in their work, fully accountable for their career progressions, and are active contributors in the growing gig-economy. And gig-economy is something that definitely deserves to be explained in more detail.

Throughout history, increase of self-employment was usually driven by high unemployment rates. So it will not come as a surprise if I told you that 10 years ago, when I shared with my parents the long-term goal to set up my own business, their immediate reaction was to ask me: "Do you feel you may become redundant in your current job?" In their careers, entrepreneurs were less-qualified people who were not able to find a solid job within the corporate world. They were struggling a lot to understand what went into me to even think about leaving a well-paid job within a safe, multinational organization. It was very difficult for them to accept that the world is changing in a direction where nothing is safe and stable any longer, and it was hard for me to vocalize properly what was so exciting about the venture I would need to build from scratch.

But from the current perspective, it is very clear that actually those years of financial crises (2008–2009) accelerated employees' interest in the gig-economy. In those years, many employees took on temporary assignments to secure any kind of income; others were able to keep a full-time job but had added some extra gigs in order to improve their overall financial situation. All in all, being able to choose flexible working hours was paramount for the evolution of the new self-employed economy, built on the premise of "talent on demand."

Ten years forward, and we can see more gig workers than ever before, usually spread across knowledge-based and service-based segments. My small consulting business would fall under the first one, and roles like drivers, writers, or various freelancing positions in marketing would be part of the second segment. One thing that is common for all of us seeking independency in our work is the fact that risk has moved away from organizations to the individual. On top of the higher risk, as my own boss, I work more hours to often earn less, but I am still more satisfied than ever in my career than before. One of the reasons for this paradox is built around the feeling that I am in the control of my choices, career, and life.

Amazing technological advancements have supported the evolution of the gig-economy for sure. But it hasn't been technology itself that was driving social changes we can observe over the past decade. Human decisions on how to organize the way we work and live were the main reasons for the change we see. Technology came as a catalyst for consolidation of those decisions and a vital support in the preparation for the world organized around personalized services.

Since my first job in 1998, I have been engaged in hiring processes around the world, and people who know me well usually say that one of my passions has always been work with the upcoming workforce. That's probably the reason that I have kept a portion of accountability for university hiring in all my roles for more than 20 years, and that passion of mine hasn't changed a bit. However, over those 20 years, graduates' career aspirations have changed enormously.

When I graduated from university, it was a common goal among my friends to find the way to get a job in a large multinational organization like IBM, Pfizer, or General Motors. Then years of financial crisis and technology booming changed the world, and so companies like Google became an ultimate dream to join for many. But needless to say, over the past couple of years, career aspirations have shifted again. In the research my team and I have conducted over the past 2 years, we have found that on average 35 percent of graduates across geographies strive to become entrepreneurs.

Those aspirations will impact the way we work in the near future. Not only that, we will need to find constructive models of collaboration between independent workers and regular employees, but we'll need to revisit the impact gig-economy will have on leadership concept we know today.

Chapter 3

Generational Battles Are Still Ongoing

I was raised in a country where family was, and still is, very important. Like in other Mediterranean countries, we were used to living and functioning in households with several generations under the same roof. It was challenging at times to keep the balance and managing very different life expectations between the generations, but, at the same time, it was a great platform to help us develop respect and high tolerance for diverse opinions, needs, and values.

In a way, every workplace is a household and every team is a family. As people live longer and retire later, for the first time in history, 5 generations of employees coexist in the workplace today. Sometimes, that coexistence can be described as a fun and exciting experience, but often it triggers issues, misunderstandings, and different views on the role work should play in our lives. Ten years ago when the entire buzz around millennials had started, I was among the people who quickly became annoyed with the whole story and attention given to the fact that a young group of people was joining our organization. Being part of the HR world, I was bombarded with advice on how to accommodate new needs, values, and behaviors that this generation was bringing into the workplace. I was clearly annoyed and often I would even openly expose my short temper with the millennial subject itself. From a distance now, I try to explain that behavior to myself, but the only reason I can find is the fact I was no longer part of the generation everyone was talking about.

Today, I am convinced that understanding different generations in the workplace is an asset that empowers us to develop high-quality relationships, form better decisions, and produce innovative solutions. It is a booster that grows our social-awareness, and it is a force that drives our ability to collaborate in various environments successfully. In this chapter, we will focus on Generations X, Y, and Z. As those 3 groups are dominating the labor market today, they will be the most represented age groups in it over the next 2 decades.

Generations are shaped by the context in which they emerge. Therefore, every generation has a different approach to work. In my case, I clearly belong to Generation X. We were born between 1960 and 1979 when everything was about capitalism and meritocracy. Hard work and effort were roads to success and good life in those years. Needless to say I was role modeling these beliefs throughout my corporate career as I was convinced that that was the only right way forward. Now I see that I just didn't know any better.

As a generation, we were individualistic in our working style and very competitive too. It was all about proving oneself and being publicly praised. That's probably the major reason why a vertical promotion was the only thing we truly cared about. In my corporate career, I was promoted every 1.6 years on average. If I would have been offered a lateral move, I would have probably been insulted and my retention risk would jump up instantly. Fast climb on the steep career ladder in large organizations was often positively related to a significant increase in our compensation packages. I dare to say, on average, we were a highly materialistic generation as well.

It was all about benefits and appearance in those days. A type of a car we droved, a title we got with a job promotion, and the size of a brand name others could see on our expensive clothes reflected on our career success and indicated our status in the society.

At the end of the 20th century, the majority of members of my generation were in the workforce, and we pushed for accelerated careers strongly. When opportunities were not obvious in our own organizations, we became open to listen to what was available outside. The war for talent had begun at that time, and our competitive habits didn't help to reduce its damage for sure. That is probably the reason why we were very vocal about different values and expectations Generation Y brought into the workplace.

Generation Y is the generation that we all like to call millennials, so I will use the same label from now on too. They were born between 1980 and 1994, at times when internet was slowly emerging and businesses around the world felt enabled to realize their global dreams. Economy was strong and stable, and purchasing power was high. Millennials brought into the workforce many novelties, but one of the most visible one was expressed in a very strong *self-orientation*. They wanted to be recognized for their achievements just like any previous generation did, but they cared about "me, myself, and I" more than the achievement itself. For the competitive members of Gen X (myself included), this was hard to digest. As young people are usually curious, millennials brought in the habit to ask everyone about anything in the organization, which was not a surprise. But what came as a surprise for many was a behavioral style in which they expressed that curiosity. Seniority and organizational hierarchy were definitely not a concern for the millennial generation, which caused various communication challenges and posed questions around values related to respect and authority.

Learning to Become a Millennial
I am a proud member of Generation X. I grew up in a time of shifting societal values, landline phones, radio, and printed newspapers. Though it may not have been a simpler time, it was certainly a less digitalized one. The emergence of social media and all the openness and transparency that accompanies it came as a shock to many of us. Not only would it drastically alter the way we communicate and socialize, it would also seriously impact our day-to-day working lives and workplace processes.

4 years ago, I was in a leading HR role in a corporate world facing significant challenges in light of the new glassdoor era. Suddenly, companies were forced to become "naked organizations" and corporate decisions and fundamental business issues became less private. They were now up for public debate and opinion. In this new age of maximized corporate transparency, workforce mobility, and severe skills shortages, it became clear to me that the future of HR, especially within leadership- and career-development areas, was in need of a rapid and drastic makeover.

This realization presented a conundrum: how could I lead this necessary HR change when I was so unprepared for the digital world myself? As far as I could see it, I was at a fork in the road and there were 2 clear career paths open to me in terms of personal and career development. I could either stay in HR roles, an area I was comfortable and experienced in, while stretching my thinking and adapting to new tools and trends. Or, I could take the road less traveled, reengineer my thinking, develop my skills, and adopt the lifestyle of the younger generation. I chose the latter option and put myself on the fast track to becoming a millennial in my early 40s.

This might sound like a peculiar statement, but let me explain my thinking. For me, "millennials" were never simply a generation. Rather, they represent a lifestyle, an attitude, and a collection of skills that we all need to develop and grow in order to stay relevant and become successful. This is something modernity demands; Generation Xers and baby boomers won't last in modern business if they are unwilling to adapt to the current environment.

There is plenty that mature professionals might learn from inexperienced colleagues, and given subsequently are the most important in my view:

They know that lifelong learning is the key to career success. As we live in a digital world of rapid technological and cultural change, we must develop transferable skills constantly to stay competitive and invest in our future. The days of when success was measured in decades of experience in a linear career pathway are over. To really learn and advance in our careers today, we need to be aware that opportunities for development might come from any direction. We need to look left, right, and below the levels of our current position—which, for my generation, can be really hard.

For many of us, fancy job titles brought the illusion of importance and security, so giving this up might be difficult. The paradox is that it is only when we step away from those benefits and feelings that we can explore liberating, rewarding, and inspiring paths toward new opportunities.

They understand the value of feedback. For the average millennial, seeking feedback is almost instinctive behavior. For me, it is not a natural impulse and I had to learn it. But once I mastered that skill, the opportunity for improvement, at both individual and interpersonal levels, became endless. I realized how important it actually is to push myself to grow and nurture my social networks. I would say it is even more important to find mentors and mentees across any age and level of seniority in our careers. Such relationships act as great mirrors for the inner-self; they are a powerful fuel for positive internal change.

They know how to share and share alike. Owning may be important, but sharing counts much more. I grew up in a culture where information was selfishly kept to oneself as a sign of power, and success was often measured in goods. Luckily, those days are long gone by. Today, we live in a world that is no longer built on assets, but access. Cars, apartments, ideas, and information that we want to share or access are available almost limitlessly.

From a career standpoint, the sharing economy drives a flexible workforce and unlocks the true value of our time, skills, and talents on a scale never before possible. The millennial generation is embracing this and using the power of information-sharing to propel their careers.

They emphasize the importance of work–life balance. The average millennial job tenure is 2 years. They are a job-hopping generation, but rather than this being reflective of a poor work ethic, it is instead indicative that millennials are constantly in search of a satisfying, purposeful job. Millennials are intrinsically motivated. They want a job to be meaningful, but they are equally passionate about their work–life balance and are also willing to sacrifice a great job to maintain this balance.

Job satisfaction and work–life balance are nonnegotiable aspects when it comes to their career paths. This is something we can all learn from. After all, the concept of earning a lot of money becomes less exciting when we know that the cost comes at our own physical, mental, and emotional well-being being put at stake.

They have the courage to commit productive failures. The courage to commit productive failures improves our career agility exponentially. Failure seems to be hardwired into adults' brains as a negative and something to be avoided at all costs. Younger generations are, by definition, more curious, courageous, and willing to take risks both in their personal and professional lives. This should not be the case. The courage to pursue change, instigate a career restart, and begin a bold new life should not be age-dependent, or the sole reserve of those with an appetite for gambling. It can, and should, be a product of a well-planned career transition based on a positive attitude and small action steps that control the level of risks.

When grounding my personal vision for the future, I have never strayed from my core strengths and values, but I let myself explore alternatives. At this point, I began investigating, searching for opportunities, and collecting valuable feedback to map my action steps toward new destinations. One small step at a time allowed me to fail without breaking my neck, and that experience set me up for bigger success. Stumbling and falling is the only way to learn how to walk. In my opinion, it's also the only way to truly accelerate our paths forward.

Today, I feel that many of us have been infected with the "millennial disease." Flexible work has become a benefit that I've started to value above any other. I care less about cars, titles, or brands—but I care more about the opportunity to learn through various experiences. It probably means that I am ready to start struggling with the new generation of upcoming workforce that has knocked on our door already.

Onboarding Generation Z

As I finally became a millennial myself, I feel ready to bring on board the newest generation that has just started to transition into workforce, and what we like to call *Generation Z*. Those guys were born between 1995 and 2010, in times of high mobility and economic instability. They have seen their parents struggling through the recession that started in 2007, and which has prompted them to think early about their own financial future. Generation Z is much more realistic than the millennials and much more cautious on how to spend and invest their money.

They were born as digital natives in neighborhoods called social networks, so they perceive the world easily through multiple realities. For the members of this generation, there is no difference between friends (and colleagues) they've met online or in the physical world, which makes them the most inclusive group in the human history.

Members of Generation Z are far less about the "me" concept and much more about the "we" approach to life. They value communities, and they seek for uniqueness in the self and others. Based on a study from 2018, McKinsey has published an article that names this youngest population in the workforce "True Gen." Findings in the study indicated strong needs for dialogue and acceptance of differences this generation demonstrates in work and life. Pragmatism, dialogue, and an exponential level of inclusion are all attributes this world badly needs. That is the reason why I am extremely excited about this new generation of colleagues at work, and I place high hopes in their opportunity to make this word a better place.

Despite their differences, millennials and Generation Zs have many similarities. Both generations care about corporate culture a lot when choosing their jobs. They want to have fun at work, flexible timings, and the opportunity to be recognized for their achievements. Both are very direct and informal in their interactions. So, in the office space for them, it's perfectly normal to approach anyone for any advice. For some "old-school leaders" that causes a lot of frustration. One criticism that is often applied to both generations is about their gaps in oral and written communication. In the world that is taken over by technological advancements, we can evidently track the decrease of empathy, social awareness, and ability to build meaningful relationships.

The good news is that both millennials and Generation Zs want to hear and accept feedback. Many surveys have shown that 40 percent of them even expect daily interactions with their managers. They want to know what they need to improve and where they can find support to do so. Needless to say, they equally expect positive reinforcement for their progress.

Continuous learning is today a requirement for all of us to stay employable. A recent study by Deloitte found that the current pace of technological change is requiring upskilling in the workplace every 2.5 years. Even scarier data come from IBM, which believes that the shelf-life of knowledge gets to only 13 months for specific industries. But, in the end, whichever number you choose to believe in, the result will be the same: in order to stay updated and relevant in our areas of expertise, we will need to learn constantly.

To stay competitive, organizations will need to become serious about the importance of being a continual learner. In my opinion, there are 2 areas that will become crucially important for the future of work and talent's progression.

1. *Social Blindness in Entry-Level Roles*
We need to reevaluate entry-level roles and the set of skills needed for successful onboarding of the emerging talent. Entry-level jobs have historically been a training ground for incoming professionals. But, as we automate more and more routine tasks, we'll indirectly reduce the need for those roles in the future, and we will require higher-order critical thinking to be developed earlier in careers.

When I speak to HR professionals and managers who regularly hire graduates, I regularly hear concerns that technology is weakening their ability to develop people skills and maintain strong interpersonal relationships among the incoming workforce. So, it is time to act. In my opinion, we should strategically invest in areas that support development of the "STEMpatheic" incoming workforce. Those will be the employees who combine strong technical knowledge needed for the future with cognitive social skills needed for successfully communication and connections with different people. Or maybe not only people?

In the future of work, we will need to be able to collaborate with machines as well. Skills like empathy, social awareness, and persuasion will become critical differentiation factors in times when artificial intelligence and the machine learning start overtaking historical human tasks. As collaboration between humans and machines grows, soft skills will become the most valuable advantage employees will need in the future. The most prominent ones will be creativity, complex reasoning, and social and emotional intelligence (EI). Unfortunately, up to now, soft skills have become a second-degree priority in formal training of traditional education. It is high time for that change to happen.

For the generation that is younger than Google, an independent and self-directed approach to learning is very important. And I personally admire that a lot. When internalized well, e-learning platforms can be a great support in onboarding initiatives to clarify formal rules and processes that exist in an organization. What they don't teach are all the cultural norms or the ways that people operate and interact in a given structure. In that particular area lies the opportunity where we can provide better support for the emerging talent that is often socially blind in their first roles.

We live in an age of self-obsession. Day in and day out, we look deep into ourselves, we seek for answers, and we try to become better parents, colleagues, partners, and leaders. But, in our personal and professional lives, our individual brilliance can't be the only arbitrator of future success. As important as self-awareness is for personal development, when we look into the workplace, it is actually social awareness that will determine whether we sink or swim.

Every organization has a culture and a certain degree of office politics. They are as much a part of office life as desks and electricity. This does not mean we all have to be big fans of office politics (I for one am not), but when we try to place ourselves above them, we limit our choice of actions and the ability to deal with them appropriately when the need arises. Therefore, I firmly believe that if we want our young talent to thrive, we need to help them learn how to navigate the business context and build sustainable networks of key relationships very early in their careers.

Social awareness, with a focus on its organizational component, should, therefore, rank highly in any corporate lexicon. Social science has a lot to say and teach us about the fact that organizational awareness is not a trait, but a skill bred from experience that can, and should, be developed as it has a strong impact on our job performance, career success, and leadership effectiveness. In other words, gaps in organizational awareness can derail the careers of otherwise intelligent, honest, hardworking people. So how can we help the raw talent in our teams compensate for their lack of experience and avoid making painful and costly mistakes?

We can harness an area of expertise in which younger generations excel. Using collaborative tools like Slack and Yammer, which look and feel similar to Facebook, allows entrants to the workplace to explore their new situation using social skills they have been honing for most of their lives. For example, while most new recruits feel intimidated at the thought of attending their first business meeting, and more than a few have committed a faux-pas or alienated a colleague through ignorance of protocol, no such feelings or lack of knowledge exist when it comes to group chats. Providing incoming workforce with the opportunity to use a highly developed set of social skills, albeit in a new context, can only be beneficial to all parties.

It is a recognized fact that the world of work is changing, but the level of our EI remains a key differentiator between star performers and the rest of the pack in every organization. The social experience and the skills we use to navigate our social environments may vary from those we used 20 years ago, but their importance for final career success has not changed a bit.

2. *Serial Learning through the On-Demand Curriculums*
It is our collective duty to create job opportunities that include mobility and variety of multidisciplinary tasks for new generations to grow. Instead of paying lip service about this subject, businesses and individuals will need to create opportunities for every employee to become a serial learner, through the available on-demand curriculums. Those organizations that will build cultures that encourage employees to become intellectually curious and to

look beyond their immediate jobs will exponentially increase their competitiveness and growth opportunities.

It is not a problem to convince the incoming workforce on how learning will be important for their career success. A recent survey in this area suggests that 45 percent of millennials and more than 50 percent of Generation Zs would rather have variety in their day-to-day job than take a promotion. It means that the new incoming workforce have started to value the breadth of experiences more than vertical progression on a career ladder. In my generation, that was not the case at all, and I am very pleased to see this shift happening.

More than half of the HR leaders I spoke with found international assignments to be an inefficient way of development for the future. They are extremely expensive and non-agile paths to leadership development. Regular shorter-term assignments (up to 3 months long) that many like to call "special projects" or task forces are increasingly popular models of generating experience. They evidently generate positive outcomes at both individual and organizational levels, which make their deployment even more relevant.

At the individual level, employees who can move beyond their regular set of tasks and next to the development of new skills also increase their visibility beyond their immediate teams. At the organizational level, special projects are becoming a way of helping innovative work get done. In this world of scarce resources we all live in, this outcome easily becomes a vital booster of energy and efficiencies in any business that aspires to grow.

But one of the challenges leaders like to throw into my face when we discuss the future of work is why to invest in continuous learning of a workforce that is job-hopping and has no loyalty for any organization. My answer is probably an oversimplified version of the only truth I see: we have no other choice! In our workforce-planning sessions (both for the short-term goals and the long-term vision), we need to factor in the motivation of our employees to regularly move between roles. Gone are the days when readiness for the next move was measured in blocks of 3–4 years, and we need to accept these new, accelerated business realities.

Not so long ago, we were commenting readiness for promotion in every talent review discussion. Today, readiness is replaced by relevance, which will bring to us a new dimension of concern. There are some sensitive, age-related debates that are already ongoing in certain industries and geographies. While in some professions, like Law and Management for example, we value accumulated experience and well-established networks; in some others—like Information and Technology—we have bias assumptions that seniority equals outdated skill sets. In order to keep the productivity high, we will need to discover innovative avenues to the future in which employees within all occupations and all age groups stay relevant and fit for their lifelong careers. That is why in chapter 6, I will be talking about concepts of career progression in the future of work, which will replace career ladders entirely.

Chapter 4

Generation Grit

This world looks young, and its size is growing superfast. More than 50 percent of the global population is currently under the age of 30, and on my birthday this year, there were 110,000 more children born than 46 years ago. But despite the size of youth around the globe, this world will get much older soon.

Already now, there are more people over the age of 65 than the age of 5. And by 2050, the share of population beyond the age of 60 will grow from the current 9 percent to around 22 percent. In March 2017, Lynda Gratton and Andrew Scott published an impressive article "The Corporate Implications of Longer Lives." Their expectation was that in case life expectancy continues to grow at the rate of 2–3 years per decade (which was the case over the last 150 years), then a child born in Japan, in 2007, will have a more than 50 percent chance of living past the age of 107. Following the same logic, children who were recently born in Switzerland or any advanced economy will have the similar odds of celebrating their 100th birthday. That thought became engraved in my brain over the past couple of years as I keep on asking myself: *will those kids ever retire?*

Greater longevity and current technological development will build the world in which the idea for education to stop at a graduation ceremony is ceasing to exist. In that world, people will not retire at the age of 65 either. In basic economic terms, it doesn't seem sustainable for the newly born generation to live well beyond 100 years and have careers shorter than 60 years. What we call a career today will look like a marathon in the not-so-distant future.

And we all know that to run a marathon successfully, one needs to be physically fit. But next to it, one equally needs to have strong perseverance for a far, long-term goal. That is why all the recently born children who we'll be onboarding into their jobs 15 years from now, I love to call Generation Grit. It is my personal coined term for the population born since 2010, and the rest of this book will be based on my own vision for the future to come. I will be looking a couple of decades into the future with an open mind to predict the world which Generation Grit will be experiencing while transitioning into the workforce. And in order to make that prediction, I would suggest that we start with a short reminder on how our world looked like 20 years ago.

Final Lessons from the Past
I still remember my excitement in 1999 about the new, upcoming millennium and the hysteria generated around the Y2K bug. Apple had launched its first iMAC, which was fixed to an office desk as in those years nothing was mobile or "on the go." Even Google was still a promising garage project, so the closest link to social media was Britney Spears, who had launched her first album and became a social phenomenon. In a word, the world felt and looked vastly different.

Flexible work didn't exist even in our ideas. Offices were usually small, dark (often cubical) spaces and in many of them it was still allowed to smoke. Majority of the work was done manually in 8-hour shifts, and loyalty (to brands and employers) was one of the core values. At the edge of the millennium, big organizations that were dominating their market space for ages started to learn serious lessons. Their size and the respective amount of business arrogance became a self-destroying machine.

Blockbuster and its ignorance of the new video-streaming trend killed the business. Their example was followed by Kodak, Nokia, and many more, who were obsessed by their glory and dreams of self-importance. "Relevance" became the buzzword of the new millennial. As the pace of change and customer's expectations were growing, many brands and businesses started to struggle to stay on top of their game. How to adapt fast and stay ahead of the competition in order to maintain the market position and growth are ever-growing concerns for any business. What can we expect to be relevant in 20 years from today is impossible to predict, but as human beings tend to repeat patterns subconsciously, I'll be brave to stretch my imagination in order to envision the future I would love to help creating.

Flashes of the Unavoidable Future
So, let's imagine for a second that we are today in 2040, and that a young girl called Sophie is keen to introduce us to the world she lives in. Sophie is a true member of Generation Grit, who is 22 years old and lives in London, UK. She was born in Dubai, and as her millennial parents were growing their careers in various geographies, she has lived in 5 different countries before her 18th birthday. Those early experiences impacted Sophie's value

system, and she grew up into a girl who loves diversity, values cultural authenticity, and insists on using technology in a smart and ethical way.

Sophie was born in 2017, as an AI native. When she was only 18 months old, she couldn't say much, but she adored the "Let It Go" song from her favorite cartoon Frozen, and she knew very well how to ask Alexa to play it over and over again. With time, Alexa and Sophie became inseparable. Alexa was there to wake her up for school, translate messages from foreign friends that Sophie met on social media, and order her a car to take her to her first date. As Sophie was getting older, Alexa was becoming smarter and capable to proactively support Sophie's needs.

Alexa was co-parenting with Sophie's full-time working mom, who was sharing her calendar with Alexa in order to be alerted about any change in activities planned for Sophie on a daily base. As much as Alexa was the irreplaceable assistant, Alexa was Sophie's best friend knowing about her in more detail than any other human being. Alexa was aware what type of clothes Sophie likes to buy, what kind of food she likes to order, what she enjoys to read on her kindle, and which kind of music she prefers on a rainy day. Being a step ahead of Sophie's needs, Alexa was able to suggest and advise Sophie with the majority of decisions she had to make through the day.

When Sophie liked a nice pair of shoes that one of her friends had recently bought, she just had to point her phone at them, and Alexa was ready to advise her about the price, producer, and esti-mated time for delivery to Sophie's home. But, as Alexa became incredibly smart, she also knew well how to remind Sophie that a similar pair of shoes was bought only a month ago, so she may consider a different color or fabric before any order was placed.

By the time Sophie was in high school, Alexa was capable to help her write the best history essay ever. Sophie was partly home-schooled as her parents were traveling and moving a lot. She had a bunch of virtual friends around the world, and she was learning how to solve problems through virtual interactions all the time. Some of Sophie's friends were Avatars, but she valued their engagement equally as with any other human friend. Language was never a barrier for them to communicate from different locations, as instant translations were provided in every platform or some channel.

Sophie was an ordinary teenager in many ways: she had a couple of million followers on social media, but she was very protective of her privacy. Unlike her millennial parents who enjoyed sharing their personal photos and life details publically, Sophie was open to share only her achievements and contributions she was making through her volunteering work. By the age of 15, many of Sophie's friends already set up their own businesses. In 2030, nobody was talking about Mark Zuckerberg as a model of unusually young entrepreneurs. For Generation Grit, it was normal to showcase the entrepreneurial spirit at a young age and set up a business venture while still in school. But none of those businesses were for profit. Members of Generation Grit were true "social warriors" on a sincere mission to turn the world into a better place.

But now in her early 20s, Sophie has graduated from a university as digital engineer and has started to think about her formal job. Over the past 10 years, Sophie had tried various gigs, where has mastered 3D-printing and design thinking. But looking into the future, Sophie wanted to learn how to collaborate with various professionals and how to lead projects of strategic importance. As much as globalization was the buzzword for Sophie's parents, in Sophie's world, everyone was talking about the space economy.

Last week, Sophie's closest friend had accepted a job offer in Washington DC, so Sophie decided to explore roles in the United States as well. She opened an account on a job-matching platform and expressed her interest for roles in the mobility ecosystem across the United States. 2 hours later, a talent broker from New York approached her and offered her a position called Chief Cyber City Analyst. Sophie actually planned to live with her friend in Washington DC, but a role in NYC would not be an issue as Hyperloop drive between the 2 cities takes only 30 minutes anyway.

You know since 2035, nobody was talking about traffic jams any more. Public transportation and self-driving cars became seamlessly connected through a mobility platform, and redundant car parks had been turned into green spaces already a while ago. Developments in urban mobility in 2030s were truly impressive, and Sophie was passionate about contributing to that progressive space. So she took a challenge and decided to explore the role.

As a Chief Cyber City Analyst, Sophie would become a team leader of a group dedicated to secure data safety used in systems and processes that enable seamless traffic functionality across New York City. That team consists of 5 analysts who have to collaborate daily with various city resilience teams. Sophie was expected to understand data flow well. From data collection to transmission and reception, all stages of data management were under her supervision as well as monitoring of her team.

The role was challenging, and it exposed Sophie to leadership that she hasn't done before. But, that was in the end not an issue. Sophie was connected to chat-boot that was providing her with any technical support needed in her job and a human mentor that helped her grow her leadership skills. There were no managers in Sophie's organization. Only teams of professionals assembled by a digital platform based on a specific project need. In that environment, leadership was not a role. Leadership was a culture of accountability where professionals take a lead in line with particular project goals, set of skills, and available resources.

Even Sophie is at the very beginning of her career; Sophie is fully accountable for its progression. She has no manager to drive that career on her behalf, and she has a sufficient set of tools to regularly measure her level of engagement in the job. At times, when that engagement falls below the acceptable threshold, Sophie is notified to initiate the transition process for the move toward the new block of roles suggested within and outside her current organization.

In 2040, talent progression is not a process that belongs to an organization anymore. It is a fully automated platform that connects individual skills, strengths, and aspirations with a dynamic job market around the world. Career progression is expected, encouraged, and rewarded, yet it is a fully regulated set of steps employees are enjoying to drive forward.

Back from the Future

Now, it is high time to wake up and get back to reality. Today, Sophie is not even 3 years old. She still lives in the Middle East, and she uses Alexa to fulfill her simple needs. Elon Musk is still exploring opportunities to build the Hyperloop, and a large number of managers are still blocking talent from their career progressions. But, the world is already moving very fast.

Progressive changes within the healthcare industry are extending human lifespan significantly. That success will inevitably increase the number of years we will be able to perform at peak capacity and consequently contribute to improvements in the society. But how to optimize our productivity, well-being, and connectivity remains to be discovered by the end of the book.

Chapter 5

Netflixization

The way we work has been disrupted for good, yet our basic talent challenges have not changed over the past 2 decades. We strive to work with superior talent because they are up to 8 times more productive than the average workforce. When managed well, the right talent is asset capable of creating huge opportunities for any business. But *where to find it* and *how to keep it* are 2 most popular questions I have been asked throughout my whole career.

Leaders around the world rank "failure to attract and retain top talent" as their key issue, ahead of any economic growth and market competitiveness. And stories about talent scarcity are horrifying. A couple of years ago, McKinsey Global Institute's study suggested that employers in Europe and North America will require 16–18 million more college-educated workers in 2020 than are going to be available. In simple words, companies may not be able to fill 10 percent of roles they need. Much less fill them with the right talent.

A whopping 82 percent of companies globally don't believe they recruit highly talented people. For companies that do, only 7 percent think they can keep it. More alarmingly, only 23 percent of managers and senior executives who are highly engaged in the talent-related topics believe their current acquisition and retention strategies will work in the near future.

I am not sure what your career aspirations were at that early age, but recent studies in this field tell me that there are some interesting developments among the "new kids on the block." At the end of 2018, Lego Group commissioned a survey of children between 8 and 12 years of age, in order to honor the 50th anniversary of the historic Apollo 11 Moon Landing. Within the study, they asked a multiple-choice question to 3,000 children in the US, UK, and China as to what they wanted to be when they grew up. They offered the children a choice of 5 professions. So, they could choose to become a musician, teacher, professional athlete, vlogger/YouTuber, or an astronaut.

Children in the US and UK had very similar answering patterns. 3 times more of them aspired to be a YouTuber (29 percent) than an astronaut (11 percent). Funnily enough, the situation in China was completely the opposite, and we may debate about the reasons behind these findings. In my personal opinion, the fact that the US nation has realized the vision to land on the moon 50 years ago may have lowered the aspirations of younger generations to be part of future attempts. Yet, despite the lack of aspiration to pursue a career in space, among children in the US and the UK, 90 percent of all assessed children had expressed their interest to learn more about space and 75 percent of them believed that humans will live in outer space and other planets, like Mars.

Honestly, I tend to agree with all of them. We all observe the race between Jeff Bezos and Elon Musk, who are competing to find the way to rocket humanity into the cosmos. Almost 20 years ago, Bezos had founded a company called Blue Origin with the vision to "create a future where millions of people are living and working in space." In May of 2019, he unveiled Blue's near-term mission to colonize the moon for exploration, science, and resource utilization. And I have no doubts that from a technical perspective, his vision may be realized sooner than we all dare to think. What keeps my brain churning is a question: where shall we source the talent for that mission to happen? I have a fear that it will not be in the US or the UK.

As everyone is saying nowadays, the future of work is here. Yet, the workforce planning for many businesses still takes place once a year through an annual budgeting cycle. That is how far we look into the future when we plan for talent needs, and that is one of the reasons that we have been complaining about the talent scarcity for more than 20 years in a row. Let's not forget that our collective success in the future of work is related to the supply of the talent we will need in the critical roles 10 years from now. And all of us being managers, parents, teachers, and leaders, we have a role to play in this game for the future at multiple levels.

I have used the survey commissioned by Lego as a metaphor and an indication of how the oversight of signals for emerging talent sent to us may impact the long-term vision the society and businesses are getting ready for. Our accountability is to pick up on those signals early in order to assess the drivers behind the new trends and through them formulate foreseeable needs. Gone are the days when workforce planning was captured on an excel sheet and also the focus on the estimated number of new hires and replacements we may have in the next year.

So, what is the solution going forward? Honestly, there is no magic I can offer on a silver plate. But I am convinced that our collective ability to envision the incoming workforce from different perspectives can help us become better prepared for the future. Recently established perks like pool tables, free lunches, and gamification-in-everything efforts are not going to be enough to attract superior talent nor keep it engaged within the same roles for long. As technological advancements are speeding up, and human hunger for personalized experiences is exponentially growing, I personally believe we should ask ourselves, "How to bring Netflixization to talent management?"

Netflix Stands for Disruption
The story tells that Reed Hastings had borrowed the *Apollo 13* movie from his local blockbuster video store and forgot to turn it back in time. Forty days later, when he finally brought the movie back, he was charged a USD40- late fee, and he got really upset. But those boiling emotions pushed Reed's brain to revisit the movie-rental business model and explore the opportunity to design a DVD-by-mail service. As a result, Netflix was founded in the August of 1997, and our story got a truly happy ending.

For me, the story about Netflix is a regular reminder that life without disruptions exists only in dreams. In order to avoid deterioration, we need to disrupt ourselves regularly, whoever we are and whatever we do. Be it managers, HR professionals, entrepreneurs, consultants, or employees in a small family business—the message is the same for all. Stretching our brains, systems, processes, and relationships is the only way to stay ahead of the curve. And when I think about talent management today, I see abundance of opportunities for disruption at various levels.

Now you may ask, but where to start? I suggest that we try to kill a CV!

The fact Leonardo da Vinci was a leading artist and intellectual of the Italian Renaissance will be of no surprise to anyone. But, while Leonardo is well remembered for his paintings, he has built one more legacy that has had a great impact on the modern world. In 1482, Leonardo produced the first *professional resume* with intent to showcase his skills. At that time, it was a handwritten document, but its main purpose did not change ever since. Almost 540 years later, and a resume is still a holy grail of every hiring process.

Businesses around the world have never done so much hiring like in the past few years. They have never spent more money in that process either. However, on a collective level, they have probably never had worse results. Resumes have impressive power to generate noise and a lot of waste. One of the graduates I met recently was proud to tell me that he has sent 186 job applications over the past month! To say that I was shocked with his statement is a massive understatement. I have tried to picture hundreds of hiring managers dealing with an application that has no matching value for the open role they had to fill and the cost this type of behavior has on the hiring industry. We have somehow allowed for a job search to turn into a lottery experience, and the cost related to that addictive habit will be very high.

When we are obsessed with resume screening and reference checking, we actually choose to look into the past. Predicting future success based on past evidence is a dangerous habit to keep. So it may be hard at times, but it's really important to move ahead with the "nonresume"-driven criteria in hiring. For me categories like cognitive ability, learning agility, resilience, and drive for achievement should be the standard to formulate our future selection decisions. Unfortunately, evidence for none of them can be found in a traditional resume. Investing into tools and technology that can improve predictions of future performance will be vital in both hiring and development efforts.

But, let's not forget that many of those apps are in early testing and immature stages, so informing ourselves well prior to any investment in this area can save us from issues along the road. Innovation is important, but the quality needs to be right. Being a psychologist I easily get excited when I see smart, young information technology profiles who believe they are capable of constructing colorful and quirky assessment tools. From the technical side, that is probably very much the truth, but from the scientific side, I have my deep concerns. Technology alone is nothing more than a processing power. The true value from AI should be found at the intersection of algorithms, deep learning, and the human insight. So in order to develop the forces that power the technology, we need to be mindful to bring psychology and social science into play from the start.

Netflix Stands for a Range of On-Demand Choices
In 2013, Netflix's leadership decided to produce their first original TV series called *House of Cards*. As a guarantee to win over new audiences, they attracted an amazing crew behind and in front of the camera. But, on top of that, they were brave to introduce another innovative move: releasing the entire season at once.

Getting instant solutions for our immediate needs is a disease that has infected all of us in this digital age. Seriously, who can even think of ordering something online and be happy to see that the delivery time is almost a week long? I know that I can't. As customers, we became impatient with every need we have and every order we place. And as business leaders or owners, we can't expect from employees to have different expectations in their jobs.

Superior talent wants to grow fast. We like to say that new generations are increasingly impatient, but it is a false assumption. The real issue is an ever-growing speed of progress that impacts our lives, needs, and expectations. To wait for a year in order to be promoted sounded like a decade in my first job. Today, it looks like a century for any graduate I speak with. The main differentiating factor between then and now is the accessibility of knowledge and the range of career alternatives we all have. Both of which will keep expanding for new generations even more.

The abundance of choices we face today is a blessing and a curse for many of us. In his book *The Paradox of Choice: Why More Is Less*, Barry Schwartz suggests how to deal with the negative impact abundance of choice has on our decision-making. He did an amazing job with explaining how the dramatic explosion in choice has paradoxically become a problem, instead of a solution. Contrary to our logic, Schwartz has developed a framework that eliminates choices in order to reduce the stress, anxiety, and busyness of our lives. And that framework is in my opinion badly needed for all of us. Did you know that 20 years ago, an average grocery store had around 7,000 items. Today, it has 50,000! So, one may think how great it is to have such a range of choice. But, in reality, when we get overwhelmed with the choice we have, we actually make no decisions and buy nothing.

We live longer, we have more opportunities to learn, and with the help of technology we generate different skills faster. When we add advancements in mobility into the mix, our career opportunities proliferate. We can choose from various jobs in various locations and various industries. Yet how do we respond in the majority of cases? We actually make no decisions and move nowhere. We become passive and delegate the accountability to our managers or career advisers, spouses, or mentors. We seek external support to help us slice those options into a size we can bite.

When I think of talent progression in the future of work, I see a massive need for solutions to reduce our range of choices and steer our attention to a final few we can choose from. Technology holds a huge potential to reduce our stress, save our time, and increase the satisfaction with the final choice we take. But before the technology is in our hands, we can improve our ability to set sights on the horizon. And we should all stop looking into a year or 2 out. The horizon stands for at least a midrange period in our lives. So setting up mid-level goals that can direct us properly toward the ultimate dream is a healthy habit gritty people practice all the time.

Netflix Stands for Data Management
Along with making their own content, from early days, Netflix invested in smart software. That investment provided them with an opportunity to track customers' watching habits and consequently generate tailor-made recommendations for further

watching. The result is simple: the smart software understands our preferences well, it provides us with a distilled range of choices, and it saves our time from searching through the generic catalogues. On top of that, the data gathered by this AI-enhanced tool provided Netflix's leaders with insights into what type of content we enjoy, so they can produce new seasons out of some old materials.

Today, data is the most valuable resource in the world—oil has lost its leading role. And it is fair to assume that our careers in the near future will not be managed by human leaders. Data management will become our crucial partner to discover environments where our potential can be realized and the context wherein we can match our strengths with aspirations to be maximized.

So, when we look for a better job or when we decide to raise money for our entrepreneurial venture, it is smart to understand what kind of skills, capabilities, and behaviors we need to display in order to convince key stakeholders that we can deliver on promise. And as entrepreneurship keeps growing, over the past decade, there were some impressive studies undertaken to discover what will drive success in situations when we pitch for investment. One of them found that *individual confidence, comfort level, and passionate enthusiasm* were the most important characteristics successful entrepreneurs had to possess to generate trust in fund raising activities.

For me this learning did not come as a surprise. In thousands of interviews I held in my career, those were the same characteristics I was valuing in candidates for open roles. And there is a strong reason behind it. When we are confident about our idea or a vision for the future, then our passionate confidence spreads out in an effortless way. It reflects our initiative, drive for achievement, hardworking attitude, persistence in the face of obstacles, and the ability to turn good ideas into opportunities. The most important element of that package comes with the fact that all those traits would be extremely hard to fake. When we try to fake confidence or enthusiasm, others can notice that something is off. Often, they can't easily articulate what is not right, but the moment doubt is part of the algorithm, the final result will be affected.

So, knowing who we are and what we want are vital ingredients of progressing toward places we want to be in. Securing those insights early in our lives will be highly important for successful talent progression in private and organizational structures alike. As long as we don't have Netflix-like models to apply, we will surf through alternative routes provided in the following chapter.

Chapter 6

Career Fitness

In the near future, we'll need to think about our skills as a bowl of milk: if we don't regularly refresh them, we'll end up with the yogurt soon! Looking back toward the old days, when we came to a college or a university, we were trained in a functional area under the assumption we would stay in it for most of our career. So, our professors at that time knew exactly what knowledge to give us. Today, we are shifting away from functional knowledge toward the ability to be fluid in our skill sets and our education. That's why, a new imperative for the universities is to teach students how to teach themselves.

Over the past 30 years, global economies went through some extraordinary developments and transformations. Companies were reengineering themselves around processes: standardizing and outsourcing those processes became a major task in order to generate higher levels of efficiency. Many markets have shifted from a manufacturing to an information society, which has caused major transitions in core employees' activities. Physical labor has been replaced with the "brain-work" that created a demand for higher levels of education and continuous training, but equally important is the new demand on our psychological resources.

At every level of the organization, employees are asked to demonstrate their capacity for self-management, accountability, self-direction, and imagination.

Did you know that the single biggest cause of work burnout is actually not driven by the work overload, but the work without personal development for a long period of time? Organizations around the world continue to spend billions of dollars in order to grow greater capabilities in their teams, and in return they expect to see continuous improvements and increased productivity. Still, the outdated design of talent-management process in many large- and medium-sized organizations fails to deliver on that expectation.

As mentioned a couple of times by now, I am a proud job-hopper. I was changing jobs and industries regularly throughout my career, but despite many moves, my resume shows how that career was at the end very narrow and linear. I have stayed in HR functionality for 20 years, and I was moving upward the traditional career ladder within a single function.

By now, I have learned that when we talk about career management, talent development, and succession planning, we usually talk about the past. The whole model based on a career ladder is likable for many years because it's based on a simple assumption that career progression follows a clear path of vertical steps over a number of years. In practice, when we want to assess talent readiness for certain positions, we normally look into their past performance and we seek for proof that they have developed the skills and the experience we've listed in our job profiles. So in a way, we believe that our past accomplishments will help us predict future success because it's much easier to remember the past than it is to imagine the future.

We are all used to a traditional 3-block model, where we study through our mid-20s, then we climb up the corporate ladder until mid-60s, and then finally we start playing golf or sipping a well-deserved cocktail on a sandy beach for as long as our health allows us. However, in the not-so-far future, in the world where people will live beyond 100 years, education and retirement will have a very different outlook. In the future of work, learning will never stop, and careers will expand into a multistaged shape of movements that we can call chapters, seasons, or even moon shots. The question that remains to be answered is how to prepare, both organizations and individuals, to drive those multi-staged careers into the future. The rest of this chapter we will dedicate to this question and explore how the role of self-management, accountability, self-direction, and imagination will play in the future of work.

Self-Management

Over the past few years, self-awareness has become a hot topic in the world of corporate HR and career coaching. Numerous books and articles have been published on the subject, and while the authors all agree that self-awareness is a prerequisite for developing leadership skills, they differ greatly in their assessment of what it actually means and how it can be developed. So, is it simply another fad or is self-awareness really something we should foster in order to get prepared for the future?

While the current obsession does seem like just another bandwagon that people are eager to jump onto (and will jump off just as quickly when the ride gets a bit bumpy), it has been my experience that the most successful individuals know who they are, what they want, and how they affect the world around them. In other words, they are self-aware.

In his legendary book *Working with Emotional Intelligence*, Daniel Goleman points to self-awareness as the cornerstone of EI. He also states that, while intelligence quotient (IQ) in the general population has risen steadily over the last 100 years, EI is clearly on the decline. This evidence has serious implications for both businesses and individuals as every wave of new entrants to the workplace is increasingly ill-equipped emotionally to handle the day-to-day demands of their jobs and demonstrate mature self-management.

Organizational psychologist Tasha Eurich in her new book *Insight* states that almost nobody is self-aware. This statement may sound exaggerated, but it is actually confirmed by studies which consistently show that we all have blind spots when judging our own abilities. In the world of self-awareness, there are 2 kinds of people: those who think they are self-aware and those who actually are.

When I teach this topic and ask the question: "Who believes that his/her self-awareness is very high," I usually get between 80 and 95 percent of hands raised up in the air. But, when I show the results of the personality assessment to those same students, usually only 20 percent of them confirm they did not get surprised with the main findings in their reports. In simple words, clear awareness of our strengths and limitations is far less realistic than we would have hoped for.

The good news, however, is that it can be developed at any age. Unlike the IQ, which changes very little after our teenage years, EI seems to be largely learned, and it continues to grow as we get older. There is an old-fashioned word for this growth in EI, and it's called maturity. Still, one thing to remember is that there are no shortcuts to self-awareness. It is not something that can be achieved overnight with the aid of pop psychology quizzes or meditation techniques. It is a continual process of development, which, according to Eurich, has 3 main steps:

The first step is a journey of self-discovery with the aim of understanding how our past experiences shape our present attitudes and aspirations and how these in turn condition our behavioral patterns and reactions. To avoid overkill with self-analysis, I strongly suggest taking a professional assessment. There are various inventories available, and since nowadays majority of them are digital, the time investment is less. For the range of choices we have, the cost should not be a blocker for accessibility either.

The second step is to establish the habit of daily reflection. The key here is to focus on asking "what" questions rather than obsessing over the "why." Again, there are no quick fixes to developing the skill of self-reflection, but at the start of the process, conversations with career counselors and trusted advisers can provide a good framework for further development.

And finally, the third step in this development should direct us to actively encourage truthful opinions on how we come across to others, even if those truths are uncomfortable. It is this last point that can cause the most difficulties in the formal work environment. In my experience, talented, high-performing employees who are on the fast lane toward leadership roles always hear how brilliant they are. People generally avoid offering critiques, especially at work. And our bosses, at the end of the day, are people as well. So they are not comfortable providing us with constructive, critical feedback, which actually opens our eyes to aspects of our behavior and its impact on other people we are not aware of.

That's why the most efficient way to accelerate our own development is to seek for external coaching support. These professionals are skilled and equipped with tools to measure how and why we behave in a certain way; they can hold the mirrors up, so we can realize what our blind spots are; and they can support us in our development efforts when times get tough. Independent and unbiased support to hack the code of self-awareness is probably the best gift we can provide to anyone who cares for success. The sooner in a career it comes, the bigger return on investment it will bring.

There are 3 core questions in the algorithm behind successful careers:

1. Who am I (what are my strengths and weaknesses)?
2. What do I really enjoy doing?
3. What skills do I have that this world needs?

The intersection of answers to those questions is the so-called career sweet spot, and it describes the zone in which we will successfully operate. When we operate in our sweet spots, we use our strengths so we feel self-confident in successful outcomes and we feel inspired to do great things. When we revisit that sweet spot in our lives regularly, we grow our chances to have a successful and fulfilled life. Here are the questions to reflect on:

Who am I? When we think about this question, it is very important to keep in mind that many of the fundamental aspects of our personality don't change—but rather they stay stable from childhood through adulthood. So we are who we are, and despite the tremendous effort we may put into development of areas where we are not strong, we may not see any significant progress over the years. What we can actually control and proactively manage instead is the environment in which we decide to play.

It is essential that we proactively evaluate and choose the right context in which we can leverage our core strengths and be focused on producing tremendous value for that given environment. This will help us build a great career, but equally enable us to turn such self-knowledge into value creation wherever we choose to apply it.

What do I enjoy doing? For me, that was always a million-dollar big question. But when I look back in my career, there were always 2 things that I not only valued, but was actually scared to lose in every job I had. The first one was the opportunity to deal with a broad range of challenges and find simple solutions for solving them. This was my so-called entrepreneurial motivation that brought me to be a business owner today. The second one was linked to my deep activism and the need to contribute in efforts to make this world a better place.

Whenever I had a feeling that I am stuck in a role which doesn't provide me with the sufficient level of challenges to be solved regularly, I've became nervous and I've started looking for the way out of that environment urgently. My short career in a bank at the very beginning of my career is a clear example of the mismatch of my personal and organizational expectations. I ran out of my first job fast, and I have never regretted that. Yet often people ask me, if it was the sign of lack of my grit in early life, and I've spent a lot of time reflecting on that question.

Today, I am certain that only very few people make career commitments in their 20s. Increasingly, we use the time in our first roles to gain valuable experiences, test our own interest, and learn how to market our core strengths. In that set up, when we decide to quit, it is definitely not a reflection of our level of grit! I would say, on the contrary, when we find areas of disconnect (which we can't have an impact on), it is wise to look for the space that will keep moving us toward our ultimate goal in a more productive way.

What skills do I have that this world needs? The answer to this question is important at any given time, but insights into skills this world will need in the future deserve to be discussed in detail. So, let's move into a debate on how to visualize the skills we expect to be scarce in the future and find the ways to be self-directed toward them today.

Self-Direction

Over the past 5 generations, workplace went through a massive set of changes. In the 19th century, most working adults were self-employed. They were selling what they had produced, and were deeply connected to their products. Self-employment was the norm and the generational expectation until the beginning of the 20th century when industrialization brought the majority of the working people into organizations. Remarkably, in just 2 generations, the society had evolved from self-employment to professional employees who exchanged their time for salaries and became significantly disconnected from the product of their labor.

The Industrial Revolution brought in bureaucracy and new expectations from work to organizations. The economy became more service-oriented, and organizations started to require efficiency and self-direction from their workforce. As a consequence, employers started to match employees' personalities to responsibilities in their job descriptions and introduced the formal planning process in their operations. With time, that process became known as the "career planning" and was designed to enable employees' professional progress. A couple of decades forward, and we were observing the rise of the internet that initiated a shift from manufacturing toward services. A move that has made the career-planning model obsolete.

Today, we are facing new expectations from work reflected in an emerging "gig" economy and holding multiple careers over a lifetime. The rapidly changing world is pressing organizations to move business modeling in which the career-planning process has fully lost its relevance. This means that the formal education process will keep on losing its relevance as well. Some of the famous names, such as Bill Gates, Anna Wintour, Mark Zuckerberg, or Ellen DeGeneres, are modern role models for the level of success only a few can match. One obvious aspect they all have in common is having no college degree. Another commonality that also links them is the fact they are all self-directed learners.

Luckily, the incoming workforce knows the value of learning well. During the last winter, I have partnered with a few business schools to assess what are the expectations of the generation that will transition into workforce this summer. The data we've collected was very clear, and showed that more than 50 percent of all assessed students valued the opportunity to learn and grow beyond any other motivator (flex work, management, financial rewards). But I still ask myself: Do they know how to steer their learning efforts toward the right set of future needs?

When you don't know where you are going, any road will take you there. But is it possible to set on the right path toward development in such a fast-moving world? Rapid technological advancements over the past decade have brought an amazing amount of requests for advanced development of basic skills and capabilities. Emerging technologies are driving radical transformation in all industries, and we are struggling to find efficient solutions to supply the sufficient set of skills that new jobs will demand in the near future.

Accountability

As individuals, we will need to learn how to manage and benefit from constant change. Our career transitions will be happening "on the go," and we will need to push ourselves out of comfort zones very consciously. I hate to say it, but we'll need to train ourselves to stretch our agility muscles regularly and learn how to manage the consequential pain successfully.

Routines can be extremely comforting as they make us calm and provide us with the sense of control. Our brain is wired to keep us away from pain and provide us with feelings of pleasure. When we're comfortable and our life feels good, our brain can release chemicals like dopamine and serotonin, which lead to happy feelings. When we are not familiar with a situation or we feel uncomfortable, then fear, stress, and anxiety will initiate the production of chemicals like adrenalin and glutamate in order to be prepared for potentially harmful situations.

More than 100 years ago, psychologists Robert M. Yerkes and John D. Dodson proved in their experiments that relative comfort creates a steady level of performance, while maximized performance is actually driven by optimal anxiety. In other words, we will achieve the peak of our performance in situations when our stress levels are a bit higher than normal. So, just outside of our comfort zone, there is the space where our mental performance and our productivity will reach its peak: the space where all the magic is waiting to happen.

Historically, the push for that jump out of the comfort zone was coming in the form of a feedback from a talent-review discussion, where our senior leaders were deciding when and where to we should move our careers. We became highly skilled in delegating the responsibility for our own success to people who had limited insights into our deep drivers, goals, and aspirations. And in the handful number of cases, what we got in return was rewarding. For the majority of employees, talent-review discussions were opportunities to start fantasizing about the great future and amazing jobs that were ahead of us.

However, our brains are really lousy in differentiating dreams from reality. When we dream, the gray substance in our brain gets relaxed and blocks our needs for action. When we don't have motivation, we do not act, we do not achieve, and at the end, we get hurt. So, when we delegate the accountability for our career development to people who have partial (and often biased) views on our core strengths, deep drivers, and aspirations, then we take the chance to stay stuck in our dreams while observing others move on.

Lately, I feel that I daily witness the career crisis of people around their 50s. The usual triggers include life changes and lack of career mobility we all would like to have. But, career crises also arise from a less obvious and deeply rooted question: Why? Where often at the age of 50 people start asking themselves questions that require sightseeing of their inner selves, it is wise to put the why aside and start asking the question as to what is the purpose we have in this world.

Our brains don't like randomness, and they are wired to try to make sense of things. Meaning is part of our operating system. In her book *The Progress Principle*, the Harvard professor Teresa Amabile discussed how meaningful work is the most-wanted element in our jobs, ahead of the salary and promotional opportunities. A healthy way for all of us to find the meaning in our lives at any age and in any job should start with the simple question: If my doctor told me that I had one more month to live, what are the top 5 things I would do?

My bucket list, as much as yours, changes regularly. The list of places I wanted to visit in my early 20s is getting shorter, while the number of lives I want to touch in the future is growing instead. That was the reason why I have decided to write this book, and this is the area where I plan to spend the next decade of my life.

I have mastered my self-awareness by now, and I am well prepared to exploit my strengths better in the future. Gone are the days when I was spending my energy in dealing with my weaknesses and waiting for passive external observers to tell me what will make me happy in life.

I personally believe that people who will strive in the future the most are going to be those who are insightful enough to spot their deep drive, brave enough to move away from zones of comfort, and creative enough to develop their own future roles.

Imagination

Dr. Daniel Gilbert is a social psychologist and the professor of psychology at Harvard University, whose work inspires my thinking regularly. His question: "Why do we make decisions that our future selves so often regret?" has urged me to look back into my own career and search for big decisions that I don't necessarily regret today, but for sure had significant impact on its overall trajectory.

When I was in my early 30s, I worked for a large tobacco industry where we had a well-established process called career development meeting (CDM), and one day after that type of a meeting, my boss told me: "We all see a great deal of potential in you and I personally believe that you should consider a general management role for the future. I am convinced that you will grow into a successful GM, in case you have the guts to step out of HR and embark on a development path within our local Sales and later on our global Marketing departments."

That path was clearly defined for the following 6- to 8-year period, and it even sounded very logical. But, as we all know by now,

I didn't have the guts! Or better to say: I lacked the imagination to push myself out of the comfort built on my life preferences and basic values at that moment in time. One thing I also did not take into account was the fact that time is an extremely powerful force. As Dr. Gilbert would say, it's a force that changes our preferences, reshapes our core values, and alters our personalities.

In my early 30s, I was clearly focused on my small personal pleasures much more than potential future successes, so I was simply blind to see myself 6–8 years out in my career. And that blindness was supported by the mighty brain that didn't play in my favor either. Neurological studies of the medial prefrontal cortex show that when we think of ourselves, this part of the brain will power up, while when we think of other people, this same part of the brain will shut down. Interestingly, when we think about our future self, our brain reacts like when we think about a complete stranger—a person that we don't know well and honestly we don't care much about. The longer the period of our imagination has to be, the less our brain will cooperate with us in order to envision the person we intend to become.

So, if our brain is sabotaging us in visualizing our future, how to subsidize the lack of imagination we may face due to valid neurological reasons? Here are some ideas to take into account:

1. Ask for the feedback regularly as people around us can mirror certain traits we have been blind-spotted to observe ourselves.
2. Dare to see the future as a nonsingular destination and challenge yourselves to build the range of choices you can consider when evaluating your potential transitions.

3. Be curious about your true motivation and revisit it regularly as it will change in different stages of your life.
4. Replace your introspective endeavors based on the question "why" with the question "how" in order to move forward and direct yourself toward the ultimate goal.
5. Tap into your past (especially those formative years of childhood) in order to create your future self—and reinvent yourself around your childhood dreams.

I regularly find amazing articles about people who have decided to shift their careers in their mid-50s. When children are out of home, and worries about basic financial security are no longer a topic, we tend to open our hearts and minds to try new things and drive our careers in new, unexpected directions. I speak to doctors who want to become marketers, navy officers transitioning into insurance business, and teachers who are setting up their consultancies. One thing they all have in common is a genuine passion for a fresh start in the second half of their career game.

Chapter 7

The Future of Leadership

The future of work is here, but the role of leadership in that future is yet to be defined. When taking a look in to the fastest growing organizations today, it's not difficult to spot that all of them are actually intense learning machines. Their leaders choose not to focus on managing, but focus on value creation instead. They understand how disrupting technologies can enable their business growth, and they are obsessed with human behavior. Insight into human patterns and drivers enables them to satisfy the needs of their customers better and engage their employees or partners behind the bold vision.

As human beings, we develop behavioral patterns every single day. It is not our conscious intent, yet patterns emerge to serve our needs. Until some pattern is actually recognized, it means there is nothing more than background noise. Luckily, our brains are wired to recognize patterns, which historically were a vital help for our precedents to detect threats and survive them. Today, in the world flooded with information, our brains need external (human and technological) support to spot existing and emerging patterns in order to produce sound decisions and form consequential actions. Pattern recognition has enormous potential for our future because it leads to innovation, new discoveries, and breakthrough disruptions.

As technology keeps ramping up, people are keen to simplify their work, increase personal time, and grow meaningful connections with other people. Increased insights into human behavior will help us all to become better entrepreneurs, partners, team members, and leaders. To be successful in future structures, we will need to learn how to collaborate with human and artificial workforces in order to navigate a shared future. But most of all, we will need to become more accountable and independent than even before.

Stumbling Blocks toward the Leadership Future
In my "futuristic conversations" with different leaders across various industries, I usually hear their aspirations to deliver on their growth targets and commitments they have toward the key stakeholders. More often than not, those aspirations are short- to mid-term based, and as our chatting brings us close to the future, the anxiety in dialogue becomes more obvious. It is hard to lead in this new, unpredictable world, and there is no doubt about it. But for many of the current and future leaders, the opportunity for future developments can be structured around 3 basic questions:

1. How to shift our focus from management toward value creation?
Success is a novelty designed in the knowledge society. As in modern times the importance of success keeps on growing, the ability to have options becomes increasingly vital. The shift

from manual work toward self-leadership massively challenges social structure. Historically, organizations were living longer than its workers, who used to be managed under strict supervision. Today, not only that human longevity is growing, but generally, the workforce doesn't need to be directed and controlled in every task they take.

And despite the rapid innovation in every aspect of our lives, at work, we often get impacted by the gravitational pull of business as usual. We are somehow better equipped with tactical solutions to deliver short-term results and please our investors than we are ready to evaluate opportunities needed to define a better future. Remaining in our day-to-day activities prevents us from exploring new paths and moving on. For anyone keen to get to the next level of performance, let me bring up here a concept called a moonshot.

In the May of 1961, American President, John F. Kennedy, issued his intent to land a man on the moon by the end of the decade. With that commitment, he connected centuries of imagination with the world of technology and human aspiration. The mission to the moon mobilized efforts of the nation throughout the decade and produced a generation of leaders on Earth.

A moonshot has the incredible power to create opportunities for identification and promotion of superb actions. In its core, it challenges us to step beyond our comfort zones and connects us with the opportunity to achieve relevant things toward a shared purpose. Within those "moonshot environments," we grow creativity and courage, we get stronger in collaborations, and we take accountability for our progress.

In a way, every start-up is a moonshot. Entrepreneurs around the world take on a moonshot without the safety net of an established organization. They are leaders who launch and pilot missions with small teams, limited resources, and short runways. That's the reason why despite their bold visions, many of them still fail, but all of them actually emerge changed and transformed by the effort itself.

Looking into the future, I believe that every leader, at leading-self and leading-others level, will need to create moonshot environments in which networks of people can thrive. To secure that value creation is coupled with reality and evidence, it will be extremely important to become obsessively connected to the customers and key partners behind the mutual mission. In that scenario, we will be stretched to upgrade our preexisting competencies, deliberately step away from our routines, and challenge our blind spots regularly. Only then, we'll be strengthening the leadership muscles and deliver excellence.

2. How to secure that change implementation happens with ease and excitement?

All of us in leadership roles today have inherited abundance of discoveries and developments within science, technology, and human behavior. Therefore, we have the chance and the obligation to utilize these assets and lead both people and businesses into a rewarding future. But change doesn't come easily, and data around the world demonstrates various levels of inability to implement it successfully.

Nokia's leadership team was extremely successful for a long time. Rightfully so, I still remember well my level when I got the

3310 model in early 2001. It was the first phone that allowed us to write long text messages, and it was superior to its competitors in all key technical parameters. By 2007, Nokia became one of the largest global organizations, worth USD150 billion. So, when in January of the same year, Steve Jobs launched his first iPhone, Nokia's leadership was very busy celebrating their own successes. But despite that, Nokia's leaders paid attention to the market situation and as always with a new launch, their engineers examined iPhone in detail. The outcome of that thorough work was a clear conclusion that iPhone was too expensive and primitive in comparison to Nokia's 3G technology. It was enough of detail for Nokia's CEO to declare how the iPhone was nothing but a niche product!

What to do when one is running a company that produces USD5.5 billion in operating profit annually and owns more than 35 percent of global smartphone market share? Should those leaders confront their shortcomings, or should they create a world where they have none? As we all very well know, Nokia's team chose the latter. It is so much easier to surround ourselves with worshipers, laugh over the critics, and minimize the touch with where the world is going. It is only natural to choose short-term strategies that boost company's stock and build their personal heroic brands. It is hard to seek long-term improvements and potentially face Wall Street's disapproval while setting the foundation for the sustainable growth over the longer haul.

In the first decade of the 21st century, many large and successful organizations experienced Nokia's model. So today we know that standing still, enjoying our current successes while underestimating the impact of the upcoming competition can demonstrate—is not acceptable. Today's leaders value competition of any size or profile and understand how the speed of change is needed in order to grow. But the pain that change requires from all of us remains the same.

We are still humans who are learning to stretch the agility muscle and who are facing the challenge to close the gap between what we genuinely want and what we are actually able to do. Not so long ago, I found some medical research that showed some mind-blowing statistics to support this statement. So in the research, it required cardiologists to confront their patients with the evidence they will literally die unless they introduce changes, like diet and exercise, to their personal lives. It was found that only 15 percent of patients were able to finally make the change. And despite such a low number, I am confident that all others still wanted to live, enjoy more holidays, and watch their grandchildren growing up. They have for sure shared the sense of urgency, and their incentives for change could not be greater. So looking into the future, how to close the "wanting–doing" gap remains to be the key learning problem in businesses and private lives alike.

It's hard to initiate behavioral change, and even harder to make it stick on. For the start, we often can't admit that we need one in the first place. Sometimes, it's because we are not even aware that a change is desirable, but more often as we could see with the cardio research, we're aware but have reasoned our way into excuses that deny our need for it. Our inner beliefs very often initiate the feeling of failure before it actually happens. These beliefs sabotage change by canceling its possibility. And we regularly hire these beliefs to justify our inaction and then wish away the result.

Stepping into the future, it is really important to consciously grow the culture of constructive feedback in everything we do. In order to create environments where change will be seen as exciting new ventures, despite the level of pain it will bring to us in the short run, we need to acknowledge that people and contexts in which we operate have powerful impacts on us. So, in order to successfully navigate the future and demonstrate the power of change that enables us to grow, we need to master our ability to anticipate, avoid, and adjust.

The importance of anticipation: in order to be successful, we can't be oblivious to the environment in which we operate. One of the most famous industries that generates masters of anticipation is law. Trial attorneys are trained to never ask a question that they don't know the answer for. Their whole approach to questioning a witness is built on anticipation. The same should apply to leadership. We should create our best environments to operate in and avoid the situation in which the external (or internal) environment starts reshaping us.

The power of avoidance: Peter Drucker, the father of management, once famously said, "Half the leaders I have met don't need to learn what to do. They need to learn what to stop." I have witnessed this saying to be true so many times in my career. Really smart, forward-looking leaders tend to fail because it takes us an enormous amount of willpower to abandon doing things we like. And successful people don't like quitting, so asking them to avoid doing something may feel like not accomplishing in tasks they want to fulfill. Yet to be successful in this fast-changing world, we may need to replace our need to always engage with the skill to selectively avoid old tricks that have lost their power.

At the end, adjustment could be a third and final luck we can explore in order to implement the change we need for the future. At times of desperate need for change, adjustments come in the form of sudden insight, advice from a coach, or a simple kick-on-our-backside. Behaviors and decisions that are highly appreciated in one environment may be completely wrong in another. Realizing subtle information and feedback from our context timely, we can steer our approach toward a more appropriate direction.

In summary, the pace of change in technology, the economy, and society is reshaping the future of work. But despite the fact that businesses have been talking loudly about accelerated change for more than a decade now, actual transformation has been, paradoxically, slow. In my opinion, we are facing an amazing opportunity to turn our leadership aspirations into future habits that will inspire the shared leadership concept to thrive. Within those shared environments, leaders will be able to complement, support, and engage each other to step up in co-creation of the future that this world is waiting for.

3. How to reduce technological blind spots?
A recent study conducted by McKinsey has found that, by 2030, there is a chance for 800 million jobs existing today to be lost. Artificial Intelligence has left the development labs and moved into our homes, offices, bars, cars, and factories. But I am nowhere close to be scared of this evolution. What keeps me awake at night is a feeling that we've started to value technology over people.

For centuries, people have been worried about machines and their effect on human lives. As machines were changing over the years, human concerns remained the same. From the first Industrial Revolution until today, we grow the fear of being displaced by technology and we block ourselves to imagine the future in which human and artificial workforce works in harmony.

One of my passions is to talk to people who work in occupations disrupted by technologies and, as you can imagine, nowadays, I talk a lot to people who we love to call "uber-drivers." It doesn't matter to me which company any of them drive for; the one thing I look for in their car is the mobile device which connects them with their customers. I always ask them the same 3 questions: do you like what you do; do you feel you are paid fairly, and what is your major concern of the near future?

As one would expect, the average answer to the first question always gets back to the feeling of freedom to work when and how they like. They feel that not having a direct boss to control them is adding value to their life, and they don't want to lose it. I usually tell them that a computer which counts the number and length of their rides seems the same like any other boss I had in my life, and in return they usually laugh at me with a comment that my bosses were for sure less fair.

When one touches the fairness of payment "uber-drivers" receive for their work, it usually becomes a more heated conversation. But that is expected. As human beings we are happy with our income for a couple of months—then our habits, lifestyle, and expectations change, and we automatically expect that our income goes up again. In general, my drivers were rational people who understood what to expect in correlation to their work, and they liked the fact they exactly know where they stand. When they need more money, they can work more and they were happy to have that trade in their own hands.

The most warring part of our chats usually comes with the last question that touches their longer-term concerns and issues they envision in their near future. Lack of self-imagination impacted by our brains becomes a serious issue to deal with. The majority usually express their concerns for their health or potential accidents on the road. But nobody sees technology as something that may impact their lives a few years down the road. While self-driving cars are on the roads testing around the world, our drivers are blind-spotted to see the threat for their occupation in the near future.

It's not only that technology is changing society; it is changing the definition of what it means to be human today. Smartphones, computers, and the Internet are revolutionary technologies, but their impact is actually no different to other big revolutions that took place over the past 1000 years. What is very different now is the shortness of time we have to assess the impacts of technologies to our lives and to adjust accordingly.

When computers arrived in the 1980s, they did not take jobs away. It was the combination of computers and fast-learning humans that took jobs away from others not being agile enough to develop new skills timely. Equally now, it is not a self-driving car itself that will hurt human drivers. It will be our inability to find areas where humans can serve as an interface between technological advancement and human needs.

At the end of 2017, Cognizant's Center for the Future of Work had published a whitepaper "21 Jobs of the Future," which declared that despite the fact work is changing, it's actually not going away. Based on the major macroeconomic, political, demographic, societal, cultural, business, and technology trends observable at that point, they have proposed 21 new jobs that will emerge over the 10–15-year period, and will become cornerstones of the future of work. Jobs like data detective, fitness commitment counselor, or chief trust officer were just a few among the 21 thoroughly described in their report, but finally all of them could be grouped under the 3 common themes: coaching, caring, and connecting.

These 3Cs were developed around the idea that no matter how technological our age becomes, humans will always seek for the human touch. So within the coaching bucket, we may find the need for jobs that will be training us, for example, how to manage our finances better. In the area of caring, we will find jobs supporting, for example, our health issues, and finally in the third C, there could be a set of jobs that would help us connect the new virtual and real worlds. I was intrigued by the whitepaper itself as in my opinion some highly innovative thinking was placed behind that work, but while I was reflecting on the suggested 3Cs, I realized that there is potentially one (4th C) missing. In my mind, the area of creating will become extremely powerful for the future of roles we as human beings may want to pursue.

Thinking about the leadership future and the structure around these 4Cs—let me step back for a second and bring us to the topic of human needs that psychologists have been studying for ages. It is impossible to talk about motivational theories without mentioning American psychologist Abraham Maslow, who developed a famous pyramid with 5 different levels of needs. From 1954, when he explained his theory in the book called *Motivation and Personality*, up-to-date, we keep on developing models that more or less overlap with his famous concept. Maslow's hierarchy of needs used the terms "physiological," "safety," "belonging and love," "social needs," or "esteem," and "self-actualization" to describe the pattern through which human motivations generally move. Explicitly, in order for our motivation to arise at the next stage, Maslow assumed that each stage must be satisfied within the individual themselves. Today, many psychologists believe that each of the 5 levels actually overlap with each other along our life spans. And I would agree with them.

Over the last 5 years, my team and I have designed an assessment tool that measures human motivators, and when we analyze thousands of data points collected by now, we can see the commonalities that allow us to group people's motivation, behind 4 main areas: people and purpose; structure and knowledge; creation and discovery; and achievements and success. Each of those areas I will describe with a bit more details:

1. People driven by "people and purpose" thrive on understanding what other people need and responding to them accordingly. They are not interested in commercial gains, but they will aspire to see that their work has a positive impact and delivers real benefits to others. Within the concept of the 4Cs, this group of people would relate well with caring. Jobs that can provide them with an opportunity to look out for others and nurture them (both through a direct and a more broad social approach) will keep them engaged and fulfilled. One of the possible roles in this area could be as a personal memory curator. As healthcare progress generates extended longevity, our seniors citizens will start to look for innovative solutions to help them bridge the fact that advances in brain-related

healthcare keep on lagging behind. This role may require consulting across a range of customers, media, and historical sources to remake and architect past experiences and reduce the stress or anxiety created by the memory loss.

2. People driven by "structure and knowledge" will seek an organized, structured, and professional environment with a clear plan so they can deliver quality work, on time and within budget. Deep knowledge and "thought leadership" are common aspirations that people in this group will share. When it comes to the concept of 4Cs, I can see people from this group being successful with coaching, mentoring, advising—the area I would call consulting. Working independently or within teams, they will feel accomplished when they can demonstrate continuous excellence of their outputs and services. In the future, space controllers will fit well into this group. As our cities constantly change due to the massive surge in drone delivery, we will need to find solutions as to how to manage our inner cities well. Once drones start occupying the sky, we'll need to not only organize flight paths but also monitor and advise how to secure zero errors that could endanger lives or properties.

3. When we think about the people who have a strong motivation behind "creation and discovery," we usually see their need to operate in environments where they are encouraged to think about issues and problems in a new and innovative way. Often, they will seek fresh approaches to their work, and will challenge the status quo regularly. In the future of work and within the 4Cs concept, this group of people will be successful in the set of jobs that call for creating. One of the future roles to think about here would be an AR journey developer. As experience

economy will keep on growing exponentially, there will be a massive need for profiles that are able to design, write, create, calibrate, and personalize the next generation of exceptional stories for customers' trips in augmented reality across various industries.

4. And finally, people driven by "achievements and success" will strive in environments that provide them with an opportunity to envision and realize business goals. Their often competitive nature comes along with the fact that they will enjoy influence, people's attention, and recognition. Therefore, going forward, their powerful social relations may be best utilized within the connecting element of the 4Cs model. What are the upcoming roles to be expected in this segment? Maybe, something that we can call a human–machine team lead? Assuming that the upcoming workforce will equally value interactions between humans and machines, we may need to anticipate the need for leadership roles capable of optimizing those interactions and experiences. The final goal for this type of roles could be the creation of hybrid teams that generate better business outcomes through human and digital collaborations.

In the conclusion of this chapter, I can't avoid to mention Warren Bennis, who was the father of contemporary leadership. He has irreversibly transformed the leadership definition from a set of personality traits we inherit in our DNA toward the result of a life-long process called self-discovery. Not so long ago, we thought about that process as a linear path toward the singular destination. Today, we are learning to accept the fact it is indefinite, collective, and it will become augmented in the not-so-distant future.

Thousands of years ago, one had to be a king to be in a position to solve large-scale problems. Hundred years ago, this power has moved into the hands of industrialists who have developed transportation systems and set up the first financial institutions. And today, we are blessed to live in a world that provides passionate and committed individuals with access to resources, technologies, and capital needed to take on any challenge. Becoming a leader of the future has never been more exciting as all of us are in a position to transfer the world's greatest challenges into the biggest business opportunities.

Pyramidal systems that value ladder-like career movements as their dominant path to better salaries, social recognition, and overall feeling of success are agility blockers at individual and organizational levels alike. If traditional leaders up to now thrived by climbing the heights of a hierarchical organization, the new generation of leaders will need to operate in a hyperconnected environment that describes growth as a collection of multidirectional transitions. How to create, grow, and nurture those ecosystems will be critically important in the near future, and I have dedicated the next chapter of this book to provide you with some frameworks and applicable ideas.

Chapter 8

The Future of Networks

Traditional leaders were focused on delivering a profitable way to run their business and secure a fine return on their people and assets. They were used to managing physical and tangible assets. Looking into the future, leaders may try to develop organizational models that will allow them to deliver their service on a truly global scale, often through virtual channels and sometimes without human teams. Knowledge in new, digital organizations lives everywhere; so, going forward, real business value will be created in relationships and networks that future leaders will be capable of generating. That is why in organizations that treat every employee as a leader, the potential for value creation will be exponential.

This shift will be hard and will not come fast, but I am certain that it is unavoidable. I was a traditional leader in my corporate career for almost 15 years. I was proudly leading HR teams around the world, and I was holding business cards with sizable titles on them. To be honest, big company names accompanied with a senior business title had the power of opening many doors for me over those years. To grab someone's attention was easy, and offers to be a keynote speaker, mentor, or a desirable prospect for the larger roles were all around me. But what defines us when that business card vanishes and one is left on her own, outside of the large corporate safety net? I can promise you, it is not the number of people reporting to us or the size of the budget we are accountable for that is important. The only thing that counted in my transition to a private venture was the network of colleagues, customers, partners, friends, and however-you-want-to-name the connections I had built over the past 20 years. In my own skin, I have experienced that the real power of me as a leader was compressed in my ability to connect employees, customers, partners, and available platforms.

Being a leader of the future will mean much more than just being able to tell a few rehearsed stories people can connect with. Don't get me wrong; storytelling is (and always will be) a very important leadership skill. But going into the exciting future led by algorithms, we will all need to master how to tear down hierarchical structures that support our internal status and instead grow and nurture the external networks.

Peter Diamandis and Steven Kotler, in 2012, published their book *Abundance: The Future Is Better Than You Think*. Today, it looks surreal how accurate some of statements are, so I will proudly reference few of their lines:

> *In today's world, what happens 'Over there' impacts 'Over here.' Pandemics do not respect borders, terrorist organizations operate on a global scale, and over-population is everybody's problem. What's the best way to solve these issues? Raise global standards of living. Research shows*

that the wealthier, more educated, and healthier a nation, the less violence and civil unrest among its populace, and the less likely that unrest will spread across its borders. As such, stable governments are better prepared to stop an infectious disease outbreak before it becomes a global pandemic.

Today, while I am writing these lines, the world is struggling to protect lives attacked by the COVID-19 virus in almost every single country. Global pandemic is on the rise forcing us to face one of the largest human tragedies in modern times. As countries are closing down their boarders and implementing strict social distancing measures, the global economy is facing a serious crisis. The world has been shacked and changed forever in only a few weeks. Many of us are on the fast track to learn what the real definition of a disruption is and what the global impact really means.

Looking at the paragraph from Peter's and Steven's book, I can't agree more that pandemics do not respect borders at all: what happened in China obviously happened in any other country in the world with only a slight delay. But, one thing that impresses me the most is the ability some governments were able to demonstrate to protect their people. Some countries managed to find effective solutions to deal with a sudden crisis; exercised social and individual accountability diligently; and utilized the power of clear, timely, and trustworthy communication well.

While governments are looking for strategies to protect the nation, businesses, large and small, are trying to survive within the newly developed environment. Effective response to a crisis usually comes in the shape of improvization, which by definition means that we need to step away from our old-fashioned beliefs that top-down communication (and the respective chain of actions) will secure business stability. It is naïve to expect that a small group of executives from the highest floor of the organizational pyramid will come up with solutions and decisions to timely deal with this volume of change. Instead, agile leaders are mobilizing their teams behind the clear set of priorities and the goal to discover and implement quick solutions for emerging problems. In order to promote problem-solving attitudes in highly chaotic conditions and under enormous levels of stress, leaders learn to operate in a network of teams.

Not so long ago, I was having a debate with leaders in one of the global biotech companies that tried to convince me how work-from-home in their organization is not possible. For years, they were rejecting every single initiative generated about the idea of flexible work. And I failed to convince them that flexible work would bring benefits into their business. The famous virus last month was completely successful in that effort. March of 2020 has introduced more changes to our workplaces than we have seen over the past 30 years. As leaders are locked-down in their homes (rather than their C-suites), they are more open to acknowledge proactive ideas from the whole team in order to deal with burning issues. Suddenly, organizations are no longer built on force, but on the collaboration glued by trust. And accountability for micro-leadership is delegated to everyone.

In small teams like mine, everyone's stake is extremely high. In case one of us is not delivering, the whole business is under threat. It doesn't matter which title we have, what "job grade" we believe we may hold, or what is the chance one of us will be promoted next year. In case one of us drops the ball, everyone is at a risk to lose the job. In the current global pandemic, we are all behind one single goal: how to reshape the service we can deliver to our clients and save the business.

In larger organizations, as the size of a team grows, the optics of the individual stake for the overall success gets smaller. Instead of growing individual accountability, we often see those teams becoming focused on individual ranks, titles, and personal benefits. And in order to grow this set of valuable perks, we tend to apply organizational politics. We spend time in self-promotion as we need to secure relevant managers having the strong visibility of our value. Our performance and results of our work are not enough—it is equally important to make sure our manager likes us enough to suggest us for promotion. But our managers are human beings who bring into the algorithm their own needs, insecurities, biases, and goals. So before we know it, we are either propelled or stuck in a career for reasons not able to be explained.

In times of a global crisis, like the one we are experiencing now, everyone is sharing the risk of exchanging a potentially fancy job title with a universally known one called "unemployed," so our collective minds rapidly become less interested in office politics. In such environments, we have the unique opportunity to find creative ways to reshape the way we operate and design future models where employees' engagement will fuel progression and growth. But who is in charge of that shaping and who should be leading the game of change? Well, by now I am convinced we all know the answer.

How to Rapidly Mobilize Troupes
We are in the war with a global pandemic. The invisible enemy that daily kills thousands of people across the world is growing stronger, and our human minds are stretched to their limits in order to find efficient solutions to win the ongoing battles. Great examples of rapid turnarounds are noticeable in every industry. Manufacturing sites that were sewing fashion clothes last month are producing sanitary equipment today; the car industry manufactures ventilators, and tobacco businesses starts growing plants that have potential to become ingredients of highly needed vaccines. Transformational efforts are visible everywhere, and nobody is scared of failing. We are all on the same mission, and for the first time in recent history, we are lined up behind a universal *moonshot* demonstrating that when we come together as one, humanity knows no limits.

Often, on an unconscious level, we are actually forming ecosystems that have the potential to survive far beyond the pandemic outbreak. We are opening up our operating systems to new and unconventional partnerships, and we are eager to explore paths less traveled in order to protect lives and jobs. As we are strengthening our defensive muscles, we are massively improving our capabilities for rapid decisions based on limited information and literally "on the go." Looking into the future, I sincerely hope that we'll be able to implement some of the learning into the way we think and behave in times of peace. Here are my 4 hopes for the future in which you, me, and the Generation Grit will be able to thrive:

1. *We will grow networks of capable and passionate professionals without organizational borders.* Can you imagine work

without bosses and hierarchy? I definitely can. I can actually clearly see the world where multidisciplinary teams are formed by an algorithm that objectively assesses people's talents, interests, and experiences. No management is needed as everyone is accountable and fully autonomous for execution of strategic goals. Yet leadership is everywhere.

In that "leader-land," people are respected for their results and collaborative efforts. Workplace is not a physical space, but rather a vibrant community of people passionate about their shared goals. It is easy to be integrated into the community as teams are used to share knowledge constantly. They are highly inclusive as everyone is required to speak up and express opinions in well-designed online forums.

And when there are no bosses, there is no organizational politics, which finally means that there may be no careers either. In "leader-land," people spend their energy to care, create, consult, and connect each other into fluid formations that allow movement in any direction at any point in time.

2. *We will learn to embrace anti-perfectionism.* In this volatile world, perfectionism is an expensive commodity. In the future, successful teams will need to apply lessons from the tech world within any industry. And those lessons are relatively simple: we need to routinely share unfinished products within relevant communities to quickly generate their feedback. One of my favorite Silicon Valley's wisdoms is the one coined by Reid Hoffman, who has established LinkedIn and who said: "If you aren't embarrassed by the first version of your product, you shipped too late!"

And recent developments caused by the global pandemic prove to us that this is all possible. For many years, I was observing education systems and their resistance to include virtual classroom options into their operating models. There was always a long list of reasons as to why it is not possible, why the time is not right, and why the quality of teaching would be deteriorated. And then, over the course of 2 weeks, we can see that schools and universities around the world are shifting their practices around 180 degrees and applying everything that until yesterday was a massive blocker of change. Is it perfect? No. Is it seamless in execution? No. But is it effective enough to move on and teach in this new environment? Oh, yes it is!

3. *We will practice emotional (not social) distancing.* In order to allow ourselves to try, fail, and regularly make mistakes, we first need to learn how to keep emotional distancing from decisions we make and choices we take. When mistakes are done, our reputation is on the line and our self-esteem may be affected. So, it is really important to learn how to properly manage our reactions and to remember that human brains are wired differently.

Brains of some people are wired to find internal reasons for everything that is going on their lives. I am one of those people. So when I make a mistake, I take the responsibility for it immediately, and I normally find personal reasons for the wrong outcome of my intents. I have no issues admitting and apologizing for that action, and I sincerely try not to repeat the same mistake. As my resilience is high, I usually manage my internal voices well, keep my self-esteem at the healthy level, and learn from those situations as much as I can.

But there are people who are emotionally so affected with every error they make that instead of thriving through the process itself, they get stuck in a zone of self-blame, sabotaging self-beliefs, and effectively blocking them from constructive learning. For this group of people, emotional distancing from results of their choices will be a vital muscle to propel their opportunities in the future of work.

4. *We will finally accept that the main purpose of every business is people.* On September 13, 1970, in *The New York Times Magazine*, Milton Friedman (an American economist who received the 1976 Nobel Memorial Prize in Economic Sciences) wrote that the social responsibility of a business is to grow profits for its shareholders. For too many years, this was the sole purpose in too many organizations around the world. But, in the future built by Generation Grit, social norms, values, and expectations will change. The sole purpose of a business will finally be its people connected through various networks of opportunities for value creation.

In the end, once we are over the pandemic threat and once our fears to satisfy basic human needs are reduced, we may find that coronavirus was one of the most simple, yet the biggest catalysts for transformation. At social, technological, and business levels alike.

When Will Our Strategy and Culture Finally Start Dating?
Over the last 20 years, Peter Drucker's statement "culture eats strategy for breakfast" was widely discussed and acknowledged. There were numerous examples of proof that no matter how strong and clear is the strategy we develop, when our values,

attitudes, and behaviors are not aligned with it, failure will be pro-gramed. But instead of explaining the obvious one more time, how about envisioning the future in which culture will take strat-egy for dinner?

One of the first projects I participated in as a management trainee many years ago was to measure culture and engagement within a bank I worked for. That survey was a well-established, bi-annual process. It was moderated by an HR, supported by a large exter-nal provider, and discussed by the executive team once results were delivered. In all other organizations I worked later, the approach was similar: employees were asked about leadership, vision, performance results, development opportunities, and their engagement level every 2–3 years. Once data was collected, results were studied for a couple of months, discussed outcomes were communicated back to the teams, and corrective actions eventually taken—at a point where engagement results arguably were simply outdated.

This is not to blame the model and the methodology I have grown with. I just believe that in the digital era, culture and engage-ment work can and should be done differently. Dynamic busi-ness environments today request fast, efficient, and user-friendly tools that provide reliable data in a timely manner. Those tools enable businesses to keep their fingers on employees' engage-ment pulses regularly and spot any negative trend early enough to deal with it proactively. Every responsible person goes for blood testing and health checkups regularly. Then, there is no reason for both leaders and employees to neglect the health of their teams either.

Walking the talk is a phrase that with years has grown in importance despite all the technological advancements we bring into the world. So, if we hope to create a world based on strong individual accountability and shared leadership models, then we need to stop micromanaging and controlling. Instead, we need to stretch our willingness to share trust, install efficient feedback loops within teams, and reward constructive failures whenever we see them. This approach in the future of work applies to all roles and all individuals. It equally applies for any project work we take and career management diligence we need to exhibit at a very personal level.

Culture is not the culprit. When organizations are in a crisis, it's usually because the business is broken. Employees are smart, educated, and dedicated people who want to be part of a successful team. They are in touch with customers daily, they see competitors from a close distance, and they get regular feedback from the ecosystem. When we establish a platform for continuous dialogue within and across teams, we invest in the development of an agile structure that can keep a business model fresh and open for spotting future opportunities.

Forward-looking leaders know that culture is not something that can be fixed. It is the evolution that takes hard work and true commitment from the whole ecosystem. However, the outcome of a strong strategy and the fully aligned culture pays off for every effort. Efficient digital tools and lean methodology can be found on many menus, and the selection is extensive. Organizations are now left to choose the best meal that will leave neither culture nor strategy hungry—a meal that calls for a next date.

Afterward: Fast Forward

For almost 30 years, I have been intrigued by human brain, behaviors, motivational drivers, and the collective power we have at hands to create value in this world. Today, I am even more impressed with the potential that can be found at the intersection of human and artificial intelligence, which is waiting to be deployed in the near future. Some of us may find this future scary and threatening, yet I personally believe that for every gritty personality, it will be nothing less but brilliant—allow me to reinforce why.

When I think about Generation Grit, I can't avoid mentioning another type of a generation that will be a driving force of technological advancements it is hard to imagine today. A fifth generation of network evolution (the so-called 5G) will bring us into a new age of hyperconnectivity. That very same hyperconnectivity will help us tap into underutilized depths of human potential in order to accelerate innovation and progress we have never seen before.

The first coffee house concept was launched in Europe in the 18th century, and it soon became a place where people would meet, share information, and initiate forward-looking ventures. As a rudimental network hub, coffee houses have survived until modern times in the form of a modern city. Roughly 75 percent of total growth takes place in urban zones where ideas are exchanged and blended in large volumes. And as much as the network established in the coffee house was small in comparison to a city, equally small is a city network compared to global connectivity.

Ten years ago, approximately 25 percent of the global population was linked to the Internet. Today, we are at 60 percent with the realistic expectation that satellite networks and the convergence of 5G will help us connect 4 billion people more. Imagine the world, only a few years away, that connects 8 billion people around the world and the potential it holds for further value creation.

The human brain is composed of 100 billion neurons and is a vital engine of our functionality. So, for more than 40 years, scientists around the world were putting efforts to discover ways as to how to utilize technology in treating patients with neurological disorders. And we are closer than ever to some extraordinary developments.

A company called Neuralink, established by Elon Musk, is on a mission to connect a patient's brain with a cloud. "Brain–Computer Interface" (BCI) technology will hopefully provide devices which can restore brain functions to patients with severe injuries and reassign them with the ability to feel and move. The most beautiful part of this innovation is expected to bring noninvasive procedure opportunities for medical doctors to treat their patients. So with a mere 2-mm slit in the skull, a robot will be able to insert hundreds of threads (meaning thousands of electrodes) into the brain's cortex within an hour-long procedure.

BCI technology has an incredible opportunity to connect memories and ideas of global population and therefore transform human intelligence for good. In my life span, this opportunity will probably be kept at a science-fiction level. But in the decades ahead of us, the true force of Generation Grit may experience the benefits of the world eager to share unfiltered emotions, innovative thoughts, and precious memories.

While in these final lines I have focused on only one technology that personally excites me a lot, but there are so many more in the pipeline getting ready to change human lives forever. Let's open our minds to embrace them and utilize their potential for the collective progression of a society that will be smarter, healthier, and happier than we can imagine.

Our role in creating a space where technology partners with human beings in an ethical, purposeful, and innovative way has been massive, and still is. This shows us that we can work toward a better world where technology and human lives are intertwined in a positive and progressive way, and there's no better time than now to make it happen. So, let's not wait for a new generation of workforce to surprise us with their beliefs, values, and working habits. Instead, let us proactively become members of a generation that will strive on the power of passion and perseverance.

About the Author

Ida Banek is a psychologist and a business leader with progressive experience in various roles, industries, and geographies. Driven by behavioral science throughout her career, she has been continually focusing on delivering efficient, solution-oriented human capital support to dynamic and fast-moving businesses. Ida uses her strong success record and high internal drive to plan and develop strategies that enable businesses to grow sustainably, deliver results consistently, and build global teams successfully.

Lightning Source UK Ltd.
Milton Keynes UK
UKHW022016081020
371257UK00007B/272